ANIMALS
IN
EARLY BUDDHISM

ARVIND KUMAR SINGH

Eastern Book Linkers

Delhi : : (India)

Published by
EASTERN BOOK LINKERS
5825, New Chandrawal, Jawahar Nagar,
Delhi-110007
Ph. : 23850287, 32919869
e-mail : ebl@vsnl.net

Edition : 2006

Price : 350.00

ISBN : 81-7854-094-0

Animals in Early Buddhism
Arvind Kumar Singh

Printed at **R.K. Print Service**, Delhi

In loving Memory of

My
Beloved Mother

Late Ahalya Singh

&

Brother-in-law

Late P.K. Singh

ACKNOWLEDGEMENTS

At the very outset, my sincere thanks to my teacher Prof. K.T.S. Sarao, who has guided me in my endeavour and not only helped me but encouraged me to write this book. He has also provided me valuable suggestions from time to time without which it would have been nearly impossible for me to complete this book.

I am also grateful to my supervisor Dr. Seema Bose for her time to time valuable assistance and able guidance.

I am also grateful to my esteemed teachers, Dr. B. Satyapala, Dr. I.N. Singh, Dr. R.K. Rana, Dr. H.P. Gangnegi and Dr. (Mrs.) Subhra Pavagadhi, with whose kind and spirited guidance I pursued my M.A., M.Phil and Ph.D. degrees from department of Buddhist Studies.

I would like to express thanks Prof. T.R. Sharma and Prof. S. K. Verma for their encouragement and support in publishing this book.

I deem it to be my paramount duty to express my sincere gratitude to my father, Prof. L.P. Singh, who encouraged and enlightened me throughout with his apt and able suggestions. I would like to express my deep gratitude to my younger brother Amitabh and his wife Chiyoko Kokubu for their moral support, encouragement and faith shown in for me. I am also grateful to my brothers, shown in Dr. Ashutosh Kumar Singh and Raja and my sisters, Mili and Varsha and the sons of my elder sister, Janu and Sanu for giving me all the encouragement and moral support which I needed during writing this book.

My humble respect and salute are absolute to all my friends, to name a few, Arunabh, Ajit, Bhuwan, Chandrashekhar Paswan, Dayanand, Kautilya, Raghavji , Rajesh Ranjan, Randhir, Subhash for their support and encouragement.

I am laso thankful to the library staffs of Central Reference Library. Arts faculty, Delhi University, Delhi, Central Library, Indian Institute of Advance Studies, Shimla (H.P.), Mannulal Central Library, Magadh University, Bodh Gaya (Bihar), for their help and assistance in completing my book. I am also thankful to Ravi Malhotra (Eastern Book Linkers) for publishing this book.

Last but not least, I am short of words to express my gratitude to my wife Kavita and my son Aryan (Kishu) who inspired me in all my work. And I am also grateful to all my well wishers, who gave me their sincere blessings in my academic life and other pursuits.

Arvind Kumar Singh

ABBREVIATIONS

A	Anguttara Nikāya
BD	Book of Discipline
BSPPB	Bihar State Pāli Publication Board
D	Digha Nikāya
DB	Dialogues of the Buddha
Dh	Dhammapada
GS	The Book of the Gradual Sayings
KS	The Book of the Kindered Sayings
J	Jātaka
JRAS	Journal of the Royal Society of India
M	Majjhima Nikāya
MLS	The Book of the Middle Length Sayings
PED	Pali English Dictionary
PTS	Pāli Text Society
S	Samyutta Nikāya
SBB	The Sacred Books of the Buddhists
SBE	The Sacred Books of the East
Sn	Sutta Nipāta
Tha	Theragāthā
Thi	Therīgāthā
Vin	Vinaya Piṭaka

CONTENTS

INTRODUCTION

If life has to reach the epitome ot its development, we must be friends to all living beings. Earnest Bell is of the view that the man who is described as behaving "like a beast" would often in his behaviour be a disgrace to any known animal. Columnist Colman McCarthy wrote. "Dismembering animals begins with dismembering language". No one can dispute animals' importance, yet we use them with an alarming lack of care. Cleveland Amory points out that we often insult each other by calling each other by animal names such as pig, swine, weasel, skunk, baboon, jackal, monkey etc. We berate each other by using animal similes such as 'mean as a snake', 'stubborn as a mule', 'crazy as a loon', 'silly as a goon'. One person ridicules another with terms like chicken, bull-headed, dumb bunny, and a questionable situation is termed 'fishy'. Derogatory words for women include, bitch, cow, shrew , vixen etc. Unthinkingly, we develop callousness and indifference towards animals by using language that is euphemistic, inaccurate and deceptive. We label the flesh we eat from animal corpses as meat, pork, veal, beef or poultry. Carol Adams is of the opinion that we have "institutionalized the oppression of animals on at least two levels which are, (i) in formal structures such as slaughter houses, meat markets, zoos, laboratories and circuses and (ii) through our language. As Colman McCarthy points out, language shapes attitudes and attitudes shape behaviours. As our society attempts to cleanse itself of it, we must become aware and get rid of this habit and adopt a vocabulary that is accurate and dignifying to animals. Animals should be given proper treatment. A long time ago, we realised that anyone who cares about the earth...really cares, must stop eating flesh of animals. Of course, anyone who cares about animals must not eat animal flesh. What strikes one most forcefully is that humankind that derives immense benefits from different creatures, not only does not give them in return the least protection but is in fact indifferent to them. The human view of the animal world has been ambivalent, a knife edge balancing of fear with fascination, affection with exploitation, kindness with cruelty, the whole complicated by theological explanations of universe and clouded by self-deciet.

The Buddha was the founder of Buddhism. He, the enlightened one, was an embodiment of mercifulness, compassion, self-love, forgiveness, truth and purity. Buddhist texts are replete with examples where animals are cared for. In Buddhism, love of animals is not sentimentality but true spirituality. Buddhism is scrupluous even in the smallest matters where either life or well being of beings is concerned. The Buddha found a profound rapport with all living beings. Buddhism believes in spiritual unity of all living creatures. It exhorts humans to befriend them. The Buddha showed a new path to humans to take a new step towards a new vision of human planetary stewardship which will become a reality only if we begin to make the right choices now, based upon *ahiṃsā* and the ethic of respect and reverence for all life.

Buddhism does not see humans as a special creation of God, or as having been given either 'dominion' or 'stewardship' over animals. Like all other sentiment beings, animals also wander in the limited, conditioned realm of *saṃsāra,* the chain of births. Nevertheless, a human rebirth is seen as a very rare and fortunate one because it is the only one where the key work for enlightenment can be accomplished. In the accounts of Buddhism, the types of rebirth are—gods, humans, animals, ghosts and hell beings where humans are listed in one group, while all other animals (land animals, birds, fish, worms, insects.)[1] are listed in another. The Buddhist *Jātaka* stories often attribute noble actions to such animals as monkeys and elephants and there is also a reference to some animals keeping the five precepts.[2]

The relatively special place of humans in the Buddhist cosmos means that they are at a high level of existence than animals. This, however, is not seen as a justification for dominating exploiting animals. Humans are 'superior' primarily in terms of their capacities for moral action and spiritual development. The natural expression of such superiority is not an exploitative attitude but one of kindness to lesser beings. One cannot isolate onseself from the plight of animals, as one has oneself experienced,[3] as animals have had past lives like humans. Moreover, in the ancient chain of rebirths, every being one comes across, down to an insect, at some time might have been a closekind relative or a good friend.[4] Bearing this in mind one should return kindness in the present state to animals.

As all sentient beings like happiness and dislike pain, however much their specific desires and sensitivities may vary, *Karniya-Mettā Sutta* speaks of radiating loving kindness to all types of beings. This is shown in one of the *Jātaka* stories[5] which concerns a bull who would pull one hundred carts to win his owner a bet only when the latter stopped using a harsh tone to get him going. Both humans and animals respond better to those who they feel are friendly, so that loving—kindness is seen to protect a person. Accordingly, the Buddha is said to have halted the charge of the rampaging elephant Nālagiri by suffusing it with loving kindness, so that it ground to a halt and bowed its head to him.[6] On another occasion, he taught that the reason a monk was bitten by a snake and had died was that he failed to radiate loving kindness to the snakes and other wild animals.[7] Animals are seen responding in a positive way to those who have a kindly presence. Once, the Buddha retired to forest to be away from some quarrelsome bhikkhus. There, an elephant and a monkey were his companions bringing him offerings.[8] In the *Theravādin* monastic code, monks are allowed to release trapped animals or fish if this is from compassion rather than a desire to steal.[9] In a more positive vein, a *Jātaka* story tells of the Bodhisattva as a hermit who, during drought, ensured that wild animals got water.[10] These sympathetic gestures and postures of early Buddhists show how much Buddhism is concerned about animals.

The present book is divided into five chapters apart from "**Introduction**" and "**Conclusion**". Chapter-I of this book is entitled "**Position of Animals in Early Buddhism**". In this chapter I have tried to show that animals have occupied a very important position in Buddhism. Unlike the *Rigveda* which regards animals as tools for human sustenace or sacrifice, the early Buddhist literatuare accords them an important place in the hierarchy of life. The importance of animals can be seen in the *Jātaka* stories of the Buddha's former lives. Of the 550 stories, a full half of them (225) have animals usually as central characters. Seventy different types of animals are mentioned and 319 animals or groups of animals appear in these 225 stories. In most of them, animals represent prior life forms of persons living at the time of the Buddha. These *Jātaka* stories illustrate the wisdom, the compassion and the moral behaviour manifested and exhibited by animals. It conveys the moral that cruelty to animals for meat and animal sacrifice are not only unethical and irreligious but also threatens the very existence of human beings. The *Jātaka* stories on animals include simple moral tales advising the Buddha's followers to avoid hurting animals intentionally. The Buddha talks about the noble acts performed by the animals. Buddhism considers animals as not animals but as potential humans or as animals that can teach humans some moral lessons.

In the this chapter we have also discussed the great acts performed by King Aśoka with regard to animal protection. The concern for animal welfare was not confined to the Buddhist monastic community but King Aśoka (274-232 BC.) converted to Buddhism and he made several laws that required kind treatment of animals, which restricted meat eating and curtailed hunting. He also established hospitals and roadside watering stations for animals.

Chapter-II of the present book is entitled "**Buddhist Concept of Ahimsa and Animal Protection**". In this chapter, I have first discussed the meaning of *ahiṃsā* and then tried my best to show how Buddhist doctrine of *Ahiṃsā* can protect animals. The positive aspect of *ahimsa* is the cultivation of goodwill and love towards all living creatures. The popular meaning of *'ahiṃsā'* is 'non-killing'. In this chapter, I have traced the origin of *ahiṃsā* to the *Rigveda* where the maturing of Hindu spirit was led to a tacit recognition of ethical primacy and religious value of *ahiṃsā*. The Buddhist doctrine of *ahiṃsā* is a moderate one and does not go to extremes. It is often expressed in phrases likes *Panatipāta Vermanī* (abstaining from injuring living creatures) and *Panatipāta Pativirati* (restraining oneself from injuring living beings). These phrases focus attention on the ethical premise concerning the value of animal lives. The Buddha condemned infliction of pain and suffering on living creature which includes humans as well as animals. He was strongly critical of the practice of animal sacrifice as well as hunting enjoyed by human beings. As mentioned in *Cakkavattisihanāda Sutta*, the ideal Buddhist ruler should provide protection not only to human beings but also to the beasts of the forests and the birds of the air (*migā-pakkhisu*).[11] This, one can say that the Buddhist concept of *ahiṃsā* is one of the most important factors which is helpful with regard to the protection of animals. The Buddha paid special attention to the important task of building up an ethical system in which justice for animals was regarded as the norm rather than the exception.

"Early Buddhist Attitude Towards Meat Eating and Animal Sacrifice" is chapter-III of the present book. In the early texts of Buddhism, it is found that the Buddha and his followers used to eat meat but on the condition that they had not seen, heard or suspected that the meat was prepared for them. This is called *Rule of the Tikotiparisuddha*. But the Buddha also allowed meat eating in some exceptional cases. For example : fat of the bear, the fish, the alligator, the swine and the ass received at right time and mixed with oil at the right time edible for the sick raw flesh and blood was permitted for the sick in diseases. Likewise, meat broth was permitted for the sick.[12] There are some meats which are not edible according to Buddhism. These are the flesh of the man, the elephant, the horse, the dog, the serpent, the lion, the tiger, the bear, the swine and the hyena.[13]

In the early texts of Buddhism, it is found that the Buddha and his disciples used to eat meat. In this chapter, I have also tried to resolve the controversy among scholars regarding the last meal taken by the Buddha himself. In this chapter, I have also discussed the steps taken by King Aśoka, the great Magadha king who was a greate follower of the Buddha and his principle of non-injury *(ahiṃsa)* to animals or any other living creatures. King Aśoka ordered not to kill any living being in his domain. He allowed the slaughter of two birds and one animal only i.e. two peacocks and one deer, whereas previously thousands of animals were being killed. Even one deer was not killed regularly and in future he hoped no animal would be killed at all.

The second section of this chapter deals with early Buddhist attitude towards animal sacrifice. I have tried my best to do justice in this section by going to all the relevant texts which deal with animal sacrifice in Buddhism. The Buddha was totally against animal sacrifice performed by the brahmanas because he was of the view that animal sacrifice did not bring rich results. On animal sacrifice he said, "Sacrifice of the horse, the man and the beast do not bring rich result. The sages do not attend a rite where diverse goats, sheep and kine are slain but sages attend to such sacrifices where no goats, sheep and kine are slain. Such rites entail great results".[14]

Chapter IV of this book is entitled **"Animal Rights and Buddhism"** where I have first discussed the origin and development of Animal Right Movement and the philosophy behind animal protection and then I have tried to relate it to Buddhism. Although history and literature record affections of human beings towards animals but no organised movement for animal welfare developed until the 19th century. The denial of a special divinity to man cleared the way for recognition not only of brotherhood to one's fellowmen but also of kinship with the animal world. The sentiment for animal protection has always existed in particular individuals. The first society for the protection of animals was formed by Richard Martin in 1824 with the name, Society for Prevention of Cruelty to Animals (SPCA). The progress of animal rights movement has been most marked in England, in the British domain and in the United States. The purpose of the earlier welfare societies was to enforce the statutes against cruelty to animals. Anti-vivisection—opposition to the use of animal sacrifice in scientific experimentation—represents a radical aspect of animal protection movement. The Buddhist ideal of non-injury to animal life clearly has implications for the use of animals in product testing and in medical research and training. From the Buddhist perspective, this might be analogous to the animal sacrifices of ancient Brahmanism. In one case, the animals were sacrificed in the name of religion and in the other, in the name of science and knowledge. In both the cases, the motive is, in part at least, to bring benefit to human beings. There is some degree of disquiet concerning the use of animals. The use of animals in medical research at least has strong utilitarian arguments in its favour. From the traditional Buddhist perspective, it is more certain that killing an animal is wrong than that generating better drugs etc. from experiments on it is good. A Buddhist point of view is that anyone prepared to do dissection and experimentation on animals has to know and accept the *kamma* of his actions. This would entail trying to do as little harm as possible, using alternative methods if available, killing only if absolutely necessary, treating the being with tender respect and making sure the knowledge is put to good use.

Chapter V of this book is entitled **"Attitude Towards Animals in Different Religions"**. We know that there is no religion without love. People may talk as much as they like about their religion but if it does not teach them to be good and kind to other animals as well as humans, it is a shame. Religion, one of whose tenets traditionally has been reverence for life (including respect for animals and the earth) is one of the strongest and most influential institutions in our society and is a guiding force for hundreds of mllions of people. As far as Christianity is concerned, it is not very supportive towards animal protection. Many zoophiles (animal lovers or those who care for animals) maintain that Christian indifference has been one of the main causes for the low status of animals. There were both negative and positive ideas and attitudes towards animals in Christianity. In Christian texts, it is found that the *Old Testament* ethics admonish that the land and the cattle which are in the service of man are to be treated as those that have their own intrinsic value and unique destiny which should not be disturbed at any cost. All creatures are to be treated as our fellow creatures and members of the community to which all human beings belong. It is of the opinion that all living beings have a right to be fruitful and multiply their kind and all of them have a rightful claim on natural resources and human beings have no right to prevent them from this claim.

To trace the Hindu attitude towards animals, one has to go back to the Vedic period and its literatuare. The Vedic deities were mostly personifications of animals forms and various animals or birds are associated with particular deities as their vehicles. In Hindu mythology, frequent occurrence of transformations of humans into animals and vice versa show the recognition that animal life is as valid as, and thus interchangeable, with, human life. On the other hand, animal sacrifice was quite prevalent in Hindu tradition at that time and is even today. The Hindus enjoyed the meat of sacrifical animals. These references in the Hindu texts shows that a great honour was shown to a guest by offering young calf's meal, though they seem to have admired the cow as a very useful animal. The idea of vegetarianism and non-violence (*ahiṁsā*) developed under the influence of Buddhism and Jainism and flourished in the 6th century B.C. though the first seeds of non-violence were sown in the *Upaniṣads*. The *Upaniṣadic* concept of all living creatures being part and parcel of Brahma emphasises the sacredness of all forms of life and thus the killing of animals is unjustifiable.

The attitude towards animals in Jainism is also dealt in this chapter. We know that the practice of *ahiṃsā* is the heart of Jainism where *ahiṃsā* means "absence of the desire to kill or harm any living creatures". In Jaina tradition, we find many instances wherethey advocate protection of animal life. Jainas respect the life of even the minutest creatures. The Islamic attitude towards animals is not like the Buddhist and the Jaina attitudes. The Islamic view is that of a harmonious relationship between human beings and the animals. Animals are not to be treated as valueless by human beings. After going through the Islamic literature, we can say that Islam is not a sentimental religion and human beings have power over the animals. In Islam, animals have practical use for the fulfilment of human desires and doing so is no sin. But on the other hand, the Prophet forbade treating animals cruelly and humans have a moral obligation towards animals. Kindness towards animals features prominently in the Jewish tradition. Causing pain to animals is not allowed and eating of animal flesh is also forbidden, though Judaism consistently values human life more than animal life.

REFERENCES

1. M. III. 167-9
2. Vin. II. 162
3. S. II. 186
4. S. II. 189-90
5. J. I. 191-3
6. Vin. II. 194-6
7. A. II. 72-73
8. Vin. I. 352-53
9. Vin. III. 62-63
10. J. I. 449-51
11. D. III. 126
12. Vin. Vol. I-VI. 10.2, Vin. 14.7
13. Vin. I. 218
14. KS. P. I. 102 (SBB)

Chapter-1

POSITION OF ANIMALS IN EARLY BUDDHISM

In Buddhist cosmology animals occupy an important niche in the categorization of realms that house humans, gods and other forms of life in an ever changing game of cosmic dance. The *Kamma* and the Rebirth are two root concepts of Buddhist philosophy and religion. According to the doctrines of *Kamma* and the Rebirth, an animal may take the same form or a different one in the next life or may even advance to human or godly status or descend to ghostly realms. Padmanabha S. Jaini in his celebrated paper entitled "Indian Perspective on the Spirituality of Animals" has cited many stories from the Buddhist, the Hindu, and the Jain traditions according to which animals do possess innate spiritual and ethical properties and capacities.[1]

The *Jataka* (Stories of Buddha's Former Births) is considered a monumental work. This includes stories connected with the previous lives of the Buddha and these stories are embedded in canonical texts. In addition to the original Pāli Gāthā, these stories include introductory content stories in which details of the identities of the animals and person including the one who was later to be reborn as the Buddha, have been enumerated in a mythical form.

There are apocryphal *Jātaka* tales as well as Aryasurya's *Jatakamala* in Sanskrit relating thirty four (34) *Jātaka* stories. *Mahāratnakūta sutta* is yet another collection of *Jātaka* stories which occupies an important position in later *Mahāyāna* texts. However, the five hundred and fifty stories related with the *Jātaka* belonging to the *Theravāda* tradition occupy the most venerable position both from the philosophical and the religious points of view. Of the 550 stories, half of them present animals as central characters. Out of 225 central animal characters of the *Jātaka,* 70 different types of animals are enumerated and 319 animals or groups of animals are mentioned in the 225 stories. Among the animals, the monkey forms the lead pack. Monkeys are represented in 27 different stories. Elephants are mentioned in 24 tales followed by Jackals (20), Lions (19), Crows (17), Deer (15), Birds (15), Fish (12) and Parrots (11). It is very interesting to note that animals represent prior life forms of persons living at the time as the Buddha. The actions of these animals throw enough light for understanding and explaining the present day human behaviour. In some cases the animal behaviour is auspicious and has laid the foundation for the auspicious human behaviour later on. In other cases, the behaviour of the animal is considered to be a bad omen and as such helps in understanding the unethical human behaviour committed by the Buddha's contemporaries, for example, the stories related to Devadutta, the cousin of the Buddha, who conspired his downfall and tried to kill the Buddha by hurling rocks at him and sending a raging elephant in his path.

These Pāli collections of the *Jātaka* stories illustrate the wisdom, the compassion and the moral behaviour manifested and exhibited by animals. These moral fables contain great philosophical and religious teachings which are of great ecological importance. They do convey the moral that cruelty to animals for meat eating and animal sacrifice is not only untethical and irreligious but threatens the very existence of homosapiens.

There are stories in *Aṅguttara Nikāya* and *Vinaya Piṭaka* which throw great light on the position of animals in *Theravāda* Buddhism. In *Vinaya Piṭaka,* it is mentioned that once the Buddha was spending *vassāvasa* at Rajgṛh and he had not enjoined upon the Bhikkhus to observe the *vassāvasa* as per the moral norms and rules. The Bhikkhus went out during the rainy season. People became very anoyed and angry. How could the Bhikkhus go on their travels during the rainy season without observing the moral norms and rules? How could a Bhikkhu belonging to the Buddhist order, go on his travels in the rainy season destroying life of many small beings, crushing the green herbs and damaging vegetable life? Buddhism believes in the Buddha nature. Every being and existence posses the Buddha nature. This is the quintessence of Buddhist philosophy and religion. Every doctrine veers round this root concept. As the story goes, the Bhikkhu conveyed the annoyance and the murmuring of the people to the Buddha. The Buddha delivered his famous address to the Bhikkhus, "I prescribe O' Bhikkhu, that you enter upon the *vassa*".[2]

Vinaya Piṭaka narrates another tale which is of great moral importance. At one time the enlightened one, the Buddha, was staying at Rajgṛh on the slopes of the Vulture's Peak. At that time a large company of monks who were friends and comrades, having made a grass hut on the *Isigili* mountain slopes, went up to live there during the rains. Also the venerable Dhaniya, the potter's son, having made a grass hut, went up to live there. Having spent the rainy season for three months, the monks demolished the grass hut, and having put away the grass and the wood, departed on tour into the country. But the venerable Dhaniya, the potter's son, spent the rainy season, the winter and the summer also there. When the venerable Dhaniya had gone into the village for alms, women gathering grass and fire wood demolished his grass hut and took away the grass and the wood. Dhaniya made a grass hut again. A second time, when he had gone into the village for alms, women gathering grass and fire wood, distroyed his grass hut and went away taking the grass and the wood. The same thing happened the third time. Then the venerable Dhaniya, the potter's son, thought : "For the third time, when I had gone into the village for alms, women gathering grass, and fire wood, demolished my grass hut and went away taking the grass and the wood. I am well taught, experienced in my craft, accomplished in the potter's craft. What if I make a hut of mud?" Then, kneading mire himself, he made a hut of mud and collecting grass and wood and cow-dung, he baked this hut. It was a beautiful, lovely, pleasing red hut.

The Buddha as he was descending from the slopes of the Vulture's Peak with a great company of monks saw this beautiful, lovely, pleasing red hut and seeing it he addresseed the monks saying :

"Bhikkhus, what is this beautiful, lovely pleasing red thing like a little lady bird *(Idogopāka)*?" Then the monks told the Buddha about it. The enlightened one, the Buddha rebuked them saying :

"Bhikkhus, it is not suitable for this foolish man, it is not fit, it is not becoming, it is not worthy of a recluse, it is not seemly, it should not be done. How, bhikkhus, can this foolish man make a hut of mud? Certainly this foolish man can have no consideration, compassion and mercy for creatures (*nāhi nāma tassa moghapurisāssa paneśu anuddaya anukaṃpā avihesa bhavissati*). Go bhikkhus, demolish this hut (*mā pacchuma janata paneśu patāvyatam apājji*). And, bhikkhus, a hut consisting of nothing but mud should not be made. Whoever shall make one, there is an offence of wrong doing".[3]

Animals have been of great significance for the preservation of environment and eco-system. Thomas Berry in his monumental work *Dream of the Earth* emphasises the importance of the protection of different species. According to him dissappearance of any species or plants from the planet earth would disturb and demolish the human consciousness. He writes :

"If we have powers of imagination, these are activated by the magic display of colour and sound, of form and movement, such as we observe in the clouds of the sky, the trees and the bushes and the flowers, the waters and the wind, the singing birds, and the movement of the greaet blue whale through the sea. If we have words with which to speak and think and commune, words for the inner experience of the divine, words for the intimacies of life, if we have words for telling stories to our children, words with which we can sing, it is again again because of the impressions we have received from the variety of beings about us".[4]

Aristotle and Descarte did not give much attention and

importance to the animal world but recent scienteific developments do attribute cognition to animals. The versatility and profundity of animals' consciousness attracted the attention of scientists who now accept and recognize an awareness and consciousness in animals that includes emotions, intentionality and to some degree logic also. Donald R. Griffin, Carolyn A. Ristau, Frans de Wall, Dorothy Cheney, Irene Pepperberg, Donald Kroodsma, and others have done pioneering scientific research on animal cognition. The weeping of elephants shows that animals also have emotions and cognitive power. A high degree of intelligence is now recognised in dolphins, chimpanzees and many other animals. Recent scientific research on animal cognition has confirmed and highlighted he Buddhist attitude towards animals as exhibited in the *Jātaka* stories.

A great debate is going on about the bio-ethical issues related with the nature and status of moral subjects. It is being debated whether only persons can be included as a moral subjects and only human beings are worthy of full moral respects or we could extend the ambit of moral concern to animal also. Buddhism takes a wider moral view than is common in the western world. Buddhism believes in the doctrine of *Kamma* according to which forms of life are interchangeable. It is accepted that over the course of time, humans can be reborn as animals and vice versa. This doctrine and belief in the interchangeable forms of life has a profound effect on the perception of the animal world. Buddhism puts emphasis on the harmony and community between humans and animals rather than highlighting the differences. It is very difficult for the western mind to accept the doctrine of interchangeable forms of life and come to terms with the idea of rebirth. However, the Buddhist canonical literature does accept the possibility of rebirth of an animal as a human and vice versa depending upon the past *Kamma*.

Animals, throughout the world, have been used as metaphors in folklores. Christopher Kay Chapple writes : "From the Anansi spider tales of the Yoruba to the Coyote sotries of North America, from the Brer Rabbit tales of the American

South to Aesop's Fables from Ancient Greece, animal stories have provided amusement, delight and wisdom for millennia. From the dawn of human history in the cave of Lascaux to the therioanthropic images of Pharaonic Egypt and Shang dynasty of China, as well as India's Indus Valley Civilization depictions of rhinocerous and various forms of cattle and cats, animals have been central to human self orientation and definition, with humans seeking in various ways to capture the power of animals to be safe from harm from animals, to feed upon animals, and through rituals to revere animals."

The Kokalīkā Jātaka tells that many years ago in Banāras, the king had a bad habit of talking too much. A wise and valued minister decided to teach the king a lesson. A cuckoo, rather than rearing her own young, had laid an egg in a crow's nest. The mother crow, thinking the egg to be one of her own, watched over the egg until it hatched and then fed the young infant bird. Unfortunately, one day, while not yet grown, the small intruder uttered the distinct call of the cuckoo. The mother crow got alarmed, pecked the young cuckoo with her beak and tossed it from her nest. It landed at the feet of the king, who turned to his minister. "What is the meaning of this?" He asked. The wise minister (the future Buddha) replied :

'They that with speech inopportune offend
Like the young cuckoo meet untimely end.
No deadly poison, nor sharp-whetted sword
Is half so fatal as ill-spoken word.'

The king, having learned his lesson, tempered his speech and avoided a possible overthrow of his rule. In his commentary, the Buddha notes that he was the wise minister and the talkative king one of his garrulous bhikkhus, Kokalīkā.[5] This story warns against taking to negative habits associated with particular animals, in this case, excessive loquaciousness.

In the *Latukīkā Jātaka*, the Buddha tells of two elephants, one the regal leader of the herd, the other a rogue marauder.[6] The head elephant one day comes upon a mother quail whose youngsters had just hatched. The quail implores the head elephant to protect her children, and he arranges for all eighty thousand of his followers to step carefully around the birds. He warns the mother quail of a rogue elephant that might come by and advises her likewise to implore him to spare her children. Despite her entreaties the rogue elephant nastily ignores the mother quail and crushes the young quail with his left foot. The mother quail, angered by the cruel murder of her brood, sets out in search of revenge. She meets with a crow, a fly, and a frog, who agree to help her. The crow pecks out the eyes of the elephant. The fly lays its eggs in the empty sockets. After the fly eggs turn into maggots and cause a frenzy of itchiness in the elephant's head, he blindly seeks out water to give him some relief. Under the guidance of the quail, the frog croaks first at the top of a mountain, leading the elephant to a precipice. He then jumps to the bottom of the cliff and croaks again. The elephant, following the sound of the frog in search of water, plunges into the chasm, and rolls to his death at the foot of the mountain. After telling this story, the Buddha states, "Brethern, one ought not to incur the hostility of anyone". He then notes that he was the friendly elephant and that Devadatta was the rouge elephant. This story, albeit gruesome in nature, warns that one must not commit random acts of destruction.

According to Buddhism, the Buddha nature is possessed by all beings. The Buddhist concept of compassion and non-violence permeates from this faith. The Buddha preached the philosophy of non-violent attitude towards even the smallest living creatures. When in Srāvasti, in the Jeta grave in the Anāthpiṇḍaka monastry, he was walking with six monks. The monks deliberately made use of water that contained living germs. The Buddha admonished the monks for deliberately using the water that contained living things. This is an offence of expiation.[7]

There is mention of another incident which shows Buddhist concern about living things. According to *Suttavibhaṅga* of *Vinaya Piṭaka*, there is a story about the Buddha living at Savatthi (Srāvasti). A bhikkhu known as Udayan, who was an archer, shot some crows and having cut-off their heads put them in a row on a stake. The Buddha was greatly moved and he scolded him for committing violence against a living creature. He said, "How can you foolish man, intentionally deprive a living creatuare of life? This is an offence of expiation."[8]

Karaniyamettā Sutta speaks of cultivation of loving kindness and compassion towards all living beings. Buddhism enjoins cultivation of goodwill towards the whole universe, boundless mind towards all living beings. *Sutta Nipāta* enjoins that a person who does not embrace compassion and non-violence and he who does not subdue baser instincts for sensual pleasures, will never again be born as a human being.[9]

The *Nandi-visāla Jātaka* highlights that kindness can tame even a wild animal. The Buddha narrated this story while he was living at Jetavana. According to the story, once upon a time, there was a king reigning at Takśīlā, the land of Gandhāra. There, the Bodhisattva took birth as a Bull. When he was a tiny calf, he was presented to a Brahman by his owners when that Brahman came to them. The Brahman called it Nandi-Visāla which means 'great joy' and treated it like his own child, feeding the young creature on gruel and rice. When the Bodhisattva became young, he thought thus to himself, "I have been brought up by this Brahman with great love, and no bull can draw what I can. How if I repay the Brahman the cost of my nurture by my strength? Accordingly, one day he said to the Brahman, "Go, Brahman, to some merchant rich in herds, and wager with him one thousand pices that your bull can draw a hundred loaded carts."

The Brahman went to a merchant who was known to own the strongest oxen in the town and said that there was no ox in the town which could pull one hundred loaded carts. The merchant said to him, "Make it a wager". "Certainly", said the Brahman, and staked one thousand pieces. Then he loaded one hundred carts with sand, gravel and stones, and leashed the lot together, one behind the other, by cords. After this, he bathed Nandi-Visāla, gave him a measure of perfumed rice to eat, hung a garland round his neck and harnessed him all alone to the leading cart. The Brahman took his seat on the cart and flourished his goad in the air, shouting "Now then, you rascal, pull them along, you rascal". "I am not the rascal he calls me", thought the Bodhisattva to himself and so he planted his four feet like so many posts, and budged not an inch.

The Brahman had to pay one thousand pieces to the merchant. His money gone, the Brahman took his bull out of the cart and went home where he lay down on his bed in grief. When Nandi-Visāla strolled in and found the Brahmana prey to such grief, he went up to him and enquired if he was taking a nap. "How could I be taking a nap, when I have had thousand pieces won of me?" "Brahman, all the time I have lived in your house, have I ever broken a pot or squeezed up against anybody, or messed about?" "Never, my child," admitted the Brahman. "Then why did you call me a rascal? It's you who are to blame, not I. Go and bet again with the merchant and this time for two thousand pieces. And only remember not to call me a rascal again." When he heard this, the Brahman went off to merchant and laid a wager of two thousand pieces. Just as before, he leashed the hundred carts to one another and harnessed the bull.

Now seated on the cart, the Brahman stroked the back of Nandi-Visāla affectionately and said "Now then, my fine fellow, pull." The Boddhisattva tugged along the whole string of the hundred carts till the hindmost stood where the foremost had started from. The merchant, rich in herds, paid up the two thousand pices he had lost to the Brahman. Other folks too gave large sums to the Bodhisattva and the whole passed into the hands of the Brahman. Thus did he gain greatly by reason of the Bodhisattva.

Thus, laying down, by way of rebuke the rule that harsh words please no one, the Master as the Buddha uttered this :

"Speak only words of kindness, never speak words unkind. For him who spoke him fair, he moved a heavy load and brought him wealth, for love."

There is another story in *Dhammapada Aṭṭhakathā* that deals with a wild elephant, Paralleyayaka who served the Buddha. The story goes like this :

The elephant mused, "Here I live, crowded by elephants, female elephants, elephant calves and young elephants. They have chewed off the tips of the grass I eat, they eat branch after branch I break down, they muddy the water I drink, whenever I plunge into or come out of the water, the female elephants come and rub against my body. Suppose I were to retire from the herd and live all alone."

So, then this noble elephant withdrew from the herd and drew néar to Paralleyayaka, to the protected forest, to the foot of the beautiful Sāl tree : even to where the Exalted one was, thither did he draw near. And when he had drawn near and paid obeisance to the Exalted one, he looked all about for a broom. And seeing none, he smote with his foot the beautiful Sāl tree below and heaved away with his trunk at the beautiful Sāl-tree above and taking a branch, he then swept the ground.

After that he took a water pot in his trunk and procured drinking water. And as hot water was required, he prepared the hot water. For this he first produced sparks with a fire-drill which he worked with his trunk and then he dropped sticks of wood on the sparks. Thus, did he kindled a fire. In the fire he first heated small stones and then he rolled it along with a stick and dropped it into a little depression in the rock. Then, he lowering his trunk and finding the water hot enough, he went and paid obeisance to the Exalted One. Then the Exalted One asked, "Is your water hot, Paralleyayaka?" And when he got the answer in affirmation, he went there and bathed. After that the elephant brought various kinds of wild fruits and presented them to the Exalted One.

Now, when the Exalted One enters the village for alms, the elephant takes his bowl and robe and then puts them on the top of his head and accompanied him. When the Exalted One reaches near the vicinity of the village, he bids the elephant bring him his bowl and robe, saying, "Paralleyayaka, further than this you are not permitted to go. Fetch me my bowl and robe just as he did before, deposits them in the teacher's place of abode, pays him the usual courtesis and fans him with the branch of a tree. At night, to ward off danger from beasts of prey, he takes a big cub in his trunk and says to himself. "I will protect the Exalted One" and back and forth he keep an eye on him whole night. When the sun rises, the elephant gives the Exalted One water herewith to wash his face, and in the manner before related performs all of the other duties.

..."Reverend Sir, what is the elephant doing?"... "Bhikkhus, having sped your parting, he desires to make me turn back," said the Exalted One to the elephant. 'Paralleyayaka, I am going now, never to return. You can't hope in this existence to enter into states of trance, or to attain spiritual insight, or the paths or the fruits. The elephant halts when he heard that and then he thrust his trunk into his mouth and retreated very slowly, weeping as he went. (Could he have made the Exalted One turn back, he would have cared for him in the very same way to the end of his days).

Now, when the Exalted One reached the vicinity of the village, he said, "Paralleyayaka, further then this it is dangerous for you to go. The habitants of the village are fraught with danger to you. The elephant halted where he was and wept. As the Exalted One slowly passed out of his sight, he died of a broken heart. Through faith in the Exalted One, he was reborn in the world of the Thirty Three in a golden mansion of thirty leagues in measure, with a retinue of a thousand celestial nymphs. God Paralleyayaka was his name.[10]

The story of the elephant, Nālagiri is directly associated with the Buddha himself. The infuriated Nālagiri was tamed by the Buddha with no other miraculous power then the power of loving kindness. This incident is narrated in *Vinaya* as follows :

There was an elephant at Rajgṛh named Nālagiri, fierce and a manslayer. Devadatta went to Rajgṛh, and to the elephant stables, and said to the elephant keepers *(Hatthi-bhanḍa)*, "I, my friends, am a relative of the king and am able to advance a man occupying a low position to a high position and to order increase of rations or of pay. Therefore, my friends, when the Buddha shall have arrived at this carriage-road (*Rakkham*), let loose the elephant Nālagiri and let him go down the road."

"Even so, Sir", said those elephant-keepers in assent to Devadatta.

The Buddha came out in the morning along with a number of Bhikkhus for alms with his bowl and robe and entered Rajgṛh and started begging. On seeing him, the elephant keepers let loose Nālagiri and let it go down the road from where the Buddha was coming. The elephant saw the Blessed One coming from the distance and as soon as it saw him, it rushed towards the Blessed One with uplifted trunk and with its tail and eaers erect.

When the Bhikkhus, who were coming along with the Blessed One, saw this, they said to the Blessed One, "This elephant, Nālagiri is fierce and a manslayer and it has got into this road. Let the Blessed One turn back, let the Happy one turn back."

"Come on, O Bhikkhus, be not alarmed. There is, O Bhikkhus, no such possilility." And a second and a third time the Bhikkhus made the same appeal and they also received the same reply.

The people climbed up to the upper storeys of their houses and to the balconies, and on to the roofs. And those of them who were unbelievers and without faith or insight, said, Truly the continence of the great Samana is beautiful but the elephant will hurt him." But those who were believers, full of devotion, able, and gifted with insight, said, "It will be long before the elephant can fight with the elephant (of men)."

And the Blessed One caused the sense of his love to pervade the elephant Nālagiri (*Mettena kittena phari*) and the elephant touched by the sense of his love lowered his trunk and went up to the place where the Blessed One was, and stood still before him, and the Blessed One stroking the elephant's forehead with his right hand, addressed him thus :

"Touch not, O elephant, the elephant of men, for sad, O elephant, is such attack, for no bliss is there, O elephant, when he is passed from hence, for him who strikes the elephant of me.

"Be not then mad, and neither be thou careless, for the careless enter not into a state of bliss. Rather, do thou thyself so act that to a state of bliss thou may go."

And Nālagiri, the elephant picked up dust with his runk from off the feet of the Blessed One and sprinkled it over its head and retired. Nālagiri returned to the stables and stood in its appointed place and became once more the tame Nālagiri. When the people saw this miraculous incident, they sang these verses :

'They can be tamed by sticks and goads and whips but the great sage has tamed this elephant without a weapon or a stick'.[11]

The understanding of *Kamma* and Rebirth prepares the Buddhists to adopt a sympathetic attitude towards animals because it is possible for human beings to be reborn in sub-human forms. *Kukkuravātika Sutta* can be cited as a canonical reference which substantiates this view. This Sutta narrated thus :

Once the Buddha was staying among the koliyans at Haliddāvaśana, the market town of the Koliyans. There an ascetic named Punna, who was a bovine ascetic (*Govā*tika), and Seniya who was an unclothed canine ascetic, having exchanged greetings with the Buddha and covered in a friendly and courteous way, sat down at a respectable distance doubling up like a dog (*Sonaka*). As he was sitting down at a respectful distance.

Thus, Panna spoke to the Buddha, "Reverend Sir, this Seniya, an unclothed canine ascetic, is a doer of things hard to do his ears lying on the ground, a canine practice which has been carried out in full by him for a long time. What is his bourn *(Gati)*, is his future state?"

"Enough, Punna, let this be, do not ask me this". And a second time ...... And a third time Punna, the Koliyan, the bovine ascetic, spoke thus to the Buddha. "Reverend Sir, this Seniya, an unclothed canine ascetic is a doer of things hard to do he eats lying on the ground, a canine which has been carried out in full by him for a long time. What is his bourn, what is his future state?"

"Although I, Punna, did not really countenance your question and said : "Enough, Punna, let this be, do not ask me this', nevertheless I will explain to you. Here Punna, some one develops the canine habits (*Kukkuraśila*) completely and constantly, he develops the canine mentality completely and constantly, he develops the canine behaviour (*kukkurakappa*) completely, and constantly. Having developed the canine practice, canine habits, canine mentality and canine behaviour completely and constantly, he on the braking up of the body after dying, arises in companionship with dogs. But if he should have a view like this : 'I' though this habit or practice or austerity or chastity (*brahmachariya*), will become a deve (*Suyama*) or a (lesser) deva' (*devānnatara*) that is a wrong view on his part. I, Punna, say that there is one of the two bourns for one of the wrong view : either Niraya hell or animal birth. So, it is Punna, that the canine practice, on prospering, leads to companionship with dogs, on failing, to *Niraya hell.*"

When this had been said, Seniya, the unclothed canine ascetic cried out and burst into burst of tears. Then the Buddha spoke thus to Punna, the Koliyan, the bovine ascetic :

'I did not countenance this (question) of yours, Punna, (so) I said : 'Enough, Punna, let this be, do not ask me this.'

"I, Revered Sir, am not crying because the lord speaks thus about me. Its, revered Sir, because this canine practice has been carried out in full by me for a long time. Revered Sir, this Punna, he Koliyan is a bovine ascetic, and the bovine practice has been carried out in full by him for a long time. What is the born, what his future state?"

"Enough, Seniya, let this be, do not ask me this, again and again. But when the Seniya, the unclothed canine ascetic thus spoke to the Buddha : "Revered Sir, this Punna, the Koliyan is a bovine ascetic, and the bovine practice has, been carried out in full by him for a long time. What is his born, what his future state?"

"Although, Seniya, I did not really countenance your (question) and said : Enough, let this be, do not ask me this, 'nevertheless I will explain to you. Here Seniya someone develops the bovine practice completely and constantly, he develops the bovine mentality completely and constantly, he develops the bovine behaviour completely and constantly. Having developed the bovine practice, mentality and hehaviour completely and constantly, he, on the breaking up of the body after dying, arises in companionship with cattle. But if he should have a view like this : 'I, through this habit or practice or austerity or chasity, will become a deva or a (lesser) deva'— that is a wrong view : either *Niraya Hell* or animal birth. So, it is, Seniya, that the bovine practice on prospering leads to companionship with cattle, on failing, to *Niraya Hell.*"

When this had been said, Punna, the Koliyan, bovine ascetic, cried out and burst into tears. Then the Buddha spoke thus to Seniya, the unclothed canine :

"I did not countenance this (question) of yours, Seniya (so) I said : Though, Seniya, let this be, do not ask me this."

"I, Revered Sir, am not crying because the Buddha speakes thus about me. It is, Revered Sir, because this bovine practice has been carried out in full by e for a long time. Revered sir, I have trust (*Paśana*) in the Buddha thus : The Buddha is able to teach Dhamma that I might give up this bovine practice and Seniya, the unclothed canine ascetics might give up that canine practice."

Well than, Punna, listen, pay carefull attention, and I will speak.

"Yes, Reversed Sir", Punna, the Koliyan bovine ascetic ansered the Buddha in assent. The Buddha thus spoke :

"Punna, these four kinds of deeds are made known by me, having realized them by my own super-knowledge. What four? There is, Punna the deed that is dark, dark in result. There is, Punna, the deed that is bright, bright in result. There is,

Punna, the deed that is dark and bright, dark and bright is result. There is, Punna, the deed that is not dark and nor bright, in result, the deed that conduces to the destruction of deeds.

And what, Punna, is the deed that is dark, dark in result? As to this, Punna someone effects (*Abhisankharoti*) an activity of body (*Kāyāsamkhāra*) that is harmful, he effects an activity of speech that is harmful, he effects an activity of mind that is harmful. He having effect an activity of body that is harmful... activity of speech that is harmful, having effected an activity of mind that is harmful, arises in a world that is harmful. Because he has appraise in a world that is harmful, harmful sensory assail him. He being assailed by harmful sensory impingement, experiences a harmful feeling, with out exception painful, even as do creatures in *Niraya Hell.* In this way, Punna, there is the uprising of a being from what has some to be (*Bhūta bhūtassa upāpati hōti*), the upraises according to what he does : when he has upraised sensory impingement assail him. So, I speak thus, Punna, creatures are heir to deeds. This Punna, is called the deed that is dark, dark in result.[12]

The Buddhist notion of merit also engenders a gentle non-violent attitude towards living creatures. It is said that if one throws dishwashing water into a pool where there are insects and living creatures, intending that they feed on the tiny particles of food thus washed away, one accumulates merit even by such trivial generosity.

It is said thus in the *Anguttara Nikāya* : Now *Vacchāgotta*, the wanderer, came to see the Exalted One.... As he sat down, *Vacchāgotta* the wanderer said this to the Exalted One :

'I have heard it said the Buddha, that the Buddha, the recluse speaks thus : "Alms should be given to me, not to others, to my followers, not to another's followers. Alms given to my followers are of great profit, no alms given to another's followers. Now, the Buddha, do they who say these things correctly repeat the views of the Buddha, without misrepresenting him by uttering an untruth? Do they expound their views in accordance with his teaching ? Indeed we are anxious not to misrepresents the Buddha.'

"Those who say so, *Vacchā*, are not of my way of thinking. Moreover, such misrepresentation of me by stating what is not true (*Asata*) is but a falsehood. Indeed, *Vacchā,* he who prevents another from giving alms, obstructs him in three ways, robs him of three things. What three?

He obstructs the giver in acquiring merit : he prevents the receivers from getting a gift and his own self is ready ruined (*Pubb' eva Kho Pan' assa atta khato*), utterly ruined. He who prevents another from giving alms, *Vacchā,* obstructs him in three way, robs him of three things. But this is what I really do declare.

Vaccha, if one should throw away pot-scouring or the rinsing of cups into a pool or cesspit, even with the idea of feeding the creatures that live therein, I declare it would be a source (*Agama*) of merit to him, to say nothing of his feeding beings that are human. Nevertheless, I say *Vacchā*, that a gift given in the case of the virtuous is of great fruit, not those given in the case of the wicked. By "virtuous" I mean one who has abandoned five qualities and possesses five qualities".[13]

There is one more story in the *Jātaka* stories named, *Macchuddana Jātaka.* According to this story, the Bodhisattva threw his left-over food into the river in order to feed the fish and by the power of this merit he was saved form an impending disaster. This story is about a dishonest merchant and it was told by the Buddha at Jatavana. The story goes like this :

Once upon a time, when Brahmadatta was the king of Benāras, the Bodhisattva was born in the family of a landed proprietor. When he grew up, he became a wealthy man. He had a young brother. After their father died, they had to manage his business. This took them to a village, where they were paid a thousand pieces of money. On their way back, as they waited on a river bank for the boat, they ate their meal. The Bodhisattva threw some food into the river (Gaṅgā) for the fishes, giving the credit to the river-spirit. The spirit accepted this with gratitude which increased her divine power. The Bodhisattva laid his upper garment upon the sand and there he lay down and went to sleep.

The younger brother was of a rather thievish nature. He wanted to filch the money from the Bodhisattva and keep it to himself. So, he packed a parcel of gravel to look like the parcel of money.

When they had got aboard and came to mid river, the younger brother deliberately stumbled against the side of the boat and by mistake dropped into the river the parcel of money believing it to be the parcel of gravel. He made it look like an accident to fool his brother.

"Brother, the money's overboard", he cried. "What's gone is gone. Never mind about it", replied the elder brother.

But the river-spirit resolved to take care of the money. So by her divine power she made a big-mouthed fish swallow the parcel and took care of it herself.

When the younger brother got home he chuckled over the trick he had played on his brother and undid the remaining parcel. There was nothing but gravel to be seen. His heart sank and he fell on his bed.

Actually, he wanted to cheat his brother by dropping into the river the parcel of gravel claiming it to be the parcel of money and keeping the money to himself. But his plan misfired.

Now some fishermen cast nets for a catch. By the power of the river-spirit, that very fish fell into the net. The fishermen took it to the town to sell. People asked the price of that big fish. "A thousand pieces and seven annas", said the fishermen. Every body made fun of them, "We have seen a fish offered for a thousand pieces". They laughed at them. The fishermen brought that fish to the Bodhisattvva's door and asked him to buy it.

"What's the price?" He asked

"You may have it for seven annas", they said.

"What did you ask other people for it?" He asked.

"From other people we asked one thousand pieces and seven annas and from you ask for seven annas only," they said.

He paid them seven annas for it and sent it to his wife.

She cut open the fish and found the parcel of money. She called the Bodhisattva. He looked at the parcel and recognising his mark knew it for his own. Then he thought that those fishermen asked other people the price of a thousand pieces and seven annas but because the thousand rupees were mine they let me have it for seven annas only.

When he had said this, he wondered how it was that he had recovered his money. At the moment the river spirit hovered invisibly in the air, and declared, "I am the spirit of the Gangā river. You gave the remains of your meal to the fishes and let me have the credit. Therefore, I have taken care of your property."

And she recited :

"You fed the fish and gave a gift to me.

This I remember and your piety".[14]

We have also found some important verses and teachings of the Buddha which deals mainly with the Buddhist attitude towards animals. These found in different Buddhist texts are as follows :

If a monk were to suffuse with love the four great snake families, he would not pass away if he were bitten by a snake. I allow you, bhikkhus, to suffuse with great love these four great snake families for the guarding of self, for the protection of self :

For the *virupākṣās* my love,

My love for the *Erāpathās*,

For the *Chabbyaputtas* my love,

And for the *Kanhāgotamakās*,

For the footless my love,

My love for the bipeds

For the four-footed my love,

My love for those with many feet.

Let not the footless do me harm,

Nor those that have two feet,
Let not the footless do me harm,
Nor those with many feet.
All creatures, all breathers,
All beings and every thing,
May they all see luck
May none came to evil.[15]

Do you see that fisherman, who, having slaughtered a haul of fish, is selling his fish-nets? I have never seen, bhikkhus, nor have I heard of such a fisherman, who, as a result of his action, as a result of his action, as a result of his mode of living, goes about on an elephant or horse or in a chariot or vehicle, or who feasts at feasts or who lives in the abundance of great wealth. Why is this? It is because he gloats evilly at fish being slaughtered or brought to slaughter. It is the same with a butcher who kills and sells cattle or sheep or swine or game or forest beasts. It is because he gloats evilly at their being slaughtered or brought to slaughter that he does not go about on an elephant or ..... live in the abundance of great wealth. Indeed, bhikkhus, he who gloats evilly at animals being slaughtered or brought to slaughter shall become neither one who goes about on an elephant ..... nor one who lives in thee abundance of great wealth. But for him who gloats evilly at a human being slaughtered or brought to slaughter, there will be woe and sorrow for a long time. At the breaking up of the body after dying, he will arise in the waste, in the Bad Bourn, in *Niraya Hell*.[16]

In many a figure would I, bhikkhus, talk a talk on animal birth, but this is as far as I go; it is not easy to describe in full, bhikkhus, so many are the woes of animal birth.[17]

How can you, foolish men, dig the rough or get some one else to do so? There are living things in the ground. Whichever bhikkhu should dig the ground or get some one else to do so, there is an offence of expiation.[18]

How can you, foolish men, fell a tree or get some one else

to do so? There are living things in a tree. There is an offence of expiation for destroying vegetable growth.[19]

Whichever bhikkhu should intentionally deprive a breathing thing of life, there is an offence of expiation.[20]

Whichever bhikkhu should make use of water knowing that it contains living things, there is an offence of expiation.[21]

Whichever bhikkhu should sprinkle water, that he knows to contain breathing things, over grass or clay or get some one else to do so, there is an offence of expiation.[22]

If a bhikkhu should make use of human flesh, there is a grave offence. A monk should not eat flesh of elephants, horses, dogs, snakes, lions, tigers, leopards, bears, hyenas, even in times of scarcity. Whoever should eat the flesh of any of these animals, there is an offence of wrong doing".[23]

The animal stories of *Jātaka* tales and other Buddhist texts include simple moral tales advising the Buddha's followers to avoid hurting animals intentionally. The Buddha tells of meritorious actions performed by animals, including remarkable acts of charity and compassion. He uses examples of the suffering of animals to sermonize against the ritual use of animals who have sacrificed their own lives to save the life of others. In Buddhism, animals are seen not so much as animals but as potential humans or as animals that can teach humans some lessons. That is why animals occupy an important place in Buddhism.

In the early Buddhist period, there was a great Buddhist King named Aśoka. The main purpose behind the mentioning of King Aśoka here is to put forward his awareness towards animals. His Edicts advise and other extensively about the well being of all creatures on this earth.

His very first Rock Edict proclaims that not a single living creature should be slaughtered and sacrificed. But he applied the royal decrees first to himself only. In the royal kitchen (*Mahānāsa*), hundreds of living creatures were slaughtered daily. King Aśoka, through his edict, limits this colossal carnage for the royal table to the killing of only two peacocks and one deer, and the deer, too, not regularly (*Nādhruvam*) and announces his intention that the slaughter of even three creatures will be stopped in future.

In this same Rock Edict, he rules out all those public entertainments which were based on cruelty to animals. The term *Samāja*, used in this edict, has been variously described in different ancient Indian texts. The Buddhist canonical text, *Digha Nikāya*, describes one of its varieties as consisting of "dancing, singing, music, story-telling, playing symbols and tom-toms". The word *Samāja* also indicates those sports and pastimes which involved violence to living creatures through contests arranged between them, such as those "between elephants, horses, buffaloes, bulls, goats and rams" "between birds like cocks and quails." Again in the *Brahmajāla Sutta* of *Digha Nikāya*, there are mentioned several objectionable shows (*Visuka-dassanam*) marked by some of the above features. These are :

(i) Nautch dances (*Nakkam*)

(ii) Singing of songs (*Gitam*)

(iii) Instrumental Music (*Veditam*)

(iv) Shows at fairs (*Pekkham*)

(v) Ballad recitations (*Akkhanam*)

(vi) hand Music (*Pānis-Saram*)

(vii) Tom-Tom playing (*Kumbhathunam*)

(viii) The chanting of Birds (*Vetalam*)

(ix) Fairy scenes (*Sobhanagārakam*)

(x) Acrobatic feats by Kandalas (*Kandālā-Vamsādhopanam*)

(xi) Combats of elephants, horses, buffaloes, bulls, goats, rams, cocks and quails.

(xii) Bouts at quarter staff, boxing and wrestling.

(xiii) Sham-fights

(xiv) Roll-calls

(xv) Manocuvres

(xvi) Reviews—the Buddha, the recluse holds aloof from visiting such shows.

Aśoka, probably, was the first king in history who provided medical treatment for men and animals alike. He did it not only in his own empire but also in the neighbouring kingdoms out of compassion. In his Rock Edict II, he orders :

"Everywhere in gods, as well as of those of his frontier sovereigns, such as the *Cholas*, the *Pandyās*, the *Satiyaputrās*, the *Keralaputrās*, as far as the *Tāmraparṇī*, the Yona king called Amtiyaka and also those who are the neighbours of Amtiyaka, everywhere has king Piyadassin, the Beloved of the gods, established medical treatment of two kinds i.e. one medical treatment for human beings and the other for animals. Wherever, medicinal herbs, wholesome for men and wholesome for animals are not found, they have everywhere been caused to be imported and planted. Roots and fruits, wherever they are not found, have been caused to be dug and trees caused to be planted for the enjoyment of man and beast."

Aśoka in his Rock Edict IV, inscribed in the twelfth year of his coronation, comments on the weak points in the administration of his predecessors and points out some wrong manners and customs of the time. According to the inscriptions, there had been a lamentable lack of regard for the sanctity of life. The result had been an increase in the slaughter of animals (*Pranārambha*) and other forms of violence, such as cruelty to the dumb creatures. Aśoka wanted to reform society of all these abuses and objectionable. By an imperial decree, the call to arms (*Bherīghosa*) was suspended and it was replaced by a call to morality (*Dhammaghosa*).

The proclamation of *Dhamma* was made by various popular exhibitions of the triumphs of religion and morality. He was of the view that these were by far less effective as means of promoting piety in people than the two novel methods introduced and tried by him, viz. imparting instruction in the law of piety or duty (*Dhammanusāthini*) and issuing the proclamation of piety (*Dhammasavanāni*).

Aśoka also claims in his Rock Edict IV that by his public instructions on morality, what was not achieved for hundreds of years been achieved i.e. increase in abstention from slaughter of animals (*Prāni*) and from violence towards all life (*Bhūta*).

Pleasure excursions (*vihārayātrā*) typified by hunting expeditions (*magavya*) were replaced by pilgrimages of piety (*Dhammayātrā*). The Rock Edict III of Aśoka mentions one of the administrative innovations which seeks to curtail even the rights of Royalty. Aśoka stopped this royal pastime. He replaced *viharayatra* by what he calls *dhammayātrā* i.e. pilgrimage for the purpose of religion.

Aśoka's Pillar Edict V gives a list of creatures which were declared protected against slaughter (*Avadhya*). Aśoka's purpose seems to have been stop for good the unnecessary killing or torture of inoffensive creatures. The abandonment of going on hunting expeditions on his part must have been in accordance with the dictates of his new religious coincidence. His intention of minimizing the slaughter of and infliction of cruelty on living beings which is clearly expressed in Rock Edict I is perceptible also behind all the restrictive measures contemplated in his regulations. The Pillar Edict V regulations are :

Parrots, mainas, adjustments (perhaps some kind of red birds), ruddy, goose, *nandi-mukhās* (an aquatic bird) and Gelatas (craves), bats, queen ants, terrapins, prawns (*Anassthika-matsyāni*), edeveyakas, *Gangāpuputakās* (a kind of fish), skate, tortoise and porcupine, tree-squirrels, *barasinga* stags, bulls set at liberty, okapinḍas (animals which find their food in houses, such as cats, mice, iguanas and mongooses) rhinoceroses, white doves, domestic doves and all quadrupeds which do not come into use, nor are eaten were not be killed.

The she goats, ewes and sows, whether with young or in milk, were not to be killed, as also their offsprings which were within six months of age. Capturing of cocks was not permitted. Husks with living beings therein were not to be burnt. Forest for nothing or for violence (to living creatures) were not to be burnt.

On the three *chaturmāsis* (i.e. on the full-moon day which falls before or after the usual season of four months) and on the *Tiśya* (i.e. Pausa Month) full moon, fish would neither be killed nor sold for three days viz., the fourteenth, the fifteenth of the first and the first of the second fortnight, as well as on all the fasting days as a rule.

On the same days, again, in the elephant forests, and in the preserves of the fishermen, other classes of living creatures would not be killed. On the eighth of every fortnight, on the fourteenth, on the fifteenth and the *Tiśya* and *Purnavasu* days, on the full moon days of the three seasons and at festivals, bulls would not be castrated, nor the goats, rams and boars nor other such animals were usually castrated.

On the *Tiśya* and *Punarvasu* days, on the full-moon days of the fortnights connected with the seasonal full-moons, the branding of horses and cows (for branding of cows, the new moon days of *Phālgun* month was considered suitable by Brahmanas) was not permitted.

Aśoka's regulations also restrained his people from killing of animals because he know that the Buddha forbade them from eating the meat of animals and particularly of those animals whose teeth had not fallen or were pregnant. This is confirmed from *Nīgrōdhamigā Jātaka* which goes thus :

Once upon a time, there was a king named Brahmadatta, The ruler of Benāras. In his kingdom, the Bodhisattva was born as a deer. At his birth he was golden of hue, his eyes were like jewels, the sheen of his horns was as of silver, his mouth was red as a bunch of scarlet cloth, his four hoods were as though lacquered, his tail was like the yak's and he was as big as a young foal. Attended by five hundred deer, he dwelt in the forest under the name of king Banyan Deer and was as golden of hue as the Bodhisattva.

In those days king Brahmadutta was passionately fond of hunting and always had meat at every meal. Every day he mustered all his subjects to the detriment of their business and went for hunting. The people thought that their work suffered because of the king and they planned to sow food and supply water for the deer in his own pleasance and having driven in a number of deer, to bar them in and deliver them over to the king. So, they sowed in the pleasance grass for the deer to eat and supplied water for them to drink and opened up the gate wide. Then they called out the people and set out into the forest armed with sticks and all manners of weapons to find the deer. They surrounded about a league of forest and in doing so surrounded the haunt of Banyan branch and deer. They started closing in and as soon as they perceived the deer, they proceeded to beat the trees, bushes and ground with their sticks till they drove the herds out of their hiding and then they rattled their swords and spears and bows with such great din that they drove all the deer into the pleasance and shut the gate. Then they went to their king and said, "Sir, you always put a stop to our work when you go for hunting, so we have driven enough deer from the forest to fill your pleasance. Henceforth feed on them.

The king betook himself to the pleasance, and in looking over them he saw among them two golden deer, to whom he granted immunity. The cook would go to the pleasance to shoot one deer but many of them were wounded in the process. The herd of deer told this to the Bodhisattva, who sent for Branch and said, "Friend, the deer are being destroyed in great numbers and though they cannot escape death, at least let them not be needlessly wounded. Let the deer go to the block by turns. One day one from my herd and the next day one from yours. Only thus thenceforth the deer whose turn it was used to go and lie down with his neck ready on the block. The cook used to go and carry off only the victim which awaited for him.

One day the lot fell on a pregnant doe of the herd of Branch and she went to Branch and said, "Lord, I am pregnant. When I have brought forth my little one, there will be two of us to take our turn. Order me to be passed over this turn." "No, I cannot make your turn another's", said he, "you must bear the consequences of your fate. Be gone." Finding no favour with him, the doe went on to the Bodhisattva and told him her story. And he answered, "Very well, you go away and I will see that the turn passes over you." And then he went himself to the place of execution and put his head on the block. When the cook saw the Bodhissatva, he cried, "What does this mean?" He knew that he had been granted immunity. So he ran off to tell this to the king. The moment the king heard of it, he mounted his chariot and arrived there with large followers. "My friend, the king of the deer, did I not promise you your life? How come that you are lying here?" The king said to the Bodhisattva.

"Sir, there came to me a pregnant doe who prayed to me to let her turn fall on another, and as I would not pass the doom of one on to another, I to lay down my life for her and taking her doom on myself."

"My lord, the golden king of the deer", said the king, "never yet saw I even among humans one so abounding in charity, love and pity as you. Therefore I am pleased with you. Arise, I spare their lives too, my lord?" Sir, only the deer in your pleasance will thus have gained immunity but what about others?" Then the king said, "Their lives too I spare, my lord". Again the Bodhisattva said, "Sir, the deer will thus be safe but what will the rest of fourfooted creatures do?" "I spare their lives too, my lord," said the king.

"Sir, four-footed creatures will thus be safe, but what about the flocks of birds?" "They too shall be spared." "Sir, birds will thus be safe but what will be the fate of the fishes, who live in water?" "I spare their lives also, my lord."

Although there is no word about the cow and her calf in Ashoka's edicts but the killing of milk cows, oxen and calves must have been out of the question because it was the custom of that time, as Vaśīṣṭha and Bodhāyana Prohibited the meat of milk-cows and oxen. Kautilya also penalized the killers of the calf, the bull and the milk cow.

Aśoka thus stands out as the pioneer of peace. He rightly recognized its foundation in the spirit and religion of universal non-violence which alone could usher in the era of "peace on Earth and Goodwill among men." His deep and delicate sensitiveness to cruelty towards animals was a matter of profound greatness.

Number of Animals Appearing in the *Jātaka* Tales

In Alphabetical Order		In Numerical Order	
Antelope	2	Monkey	27
Bear	1	Elephant	24
Beetle	1	Jackal	20
Bird	15	Lion	19
Boar	5	Crow	17
Buffalo	1	Bird	15
Bull	4	Deer, stag, doe	15
Cat	1	Fish	12
Chameleon	2	Parrot	11
Chicken	2	Snake	10
Cow	3	Tree spirit	10
Crab	3	Horse	8
Crane	3	Goose	7
Crocodile	4	Tiger	7
Crow	17	Tortoise	7
Cuckoo	3	Boar	5
Deer, stag, doe	15	Goat	5
Dog	4	Quail	5
Donkey	2	Bull	4
Duck	1	Crocodile	4
Eagle	1	Dog	4
Elephant	24	Ox	4
Elk	1	Partridge	4
Falcon	2	Peacock	4
Fish	12	Rat	4
Fly	1	Vulture	4
Fox	1	Cow	3
Frog	1	Crab	3
Goat	5	Crane	3
Goose	7	Cuckoo	3
Grass spirit	1	Lizard	3
Hawk	1	Pig	3
Horse	8	Pigeon	3
Hound	1	Serpent	3
Iguana	1	Woodpecker	3

Jackal	20	Antelope	2
Jay	1	Chameleon	2
Lion	19	Chicken	2
Lizard	3	Donkey	2
Mongoose	1	Falcon	2
Monkey	27	Osprey	2
Mosquito	1	Owl	2
Mouse	1	Rabbit	2
Osprey	2	Rooster	2
Otter	1	Viper	2
Owl	2	Water spirit	2
Ox	4	Bear	1
Panther	1	Beetle	1
Parrot	11	Buffalo	1
Pattridge	4	Cat	1
Peacock	4	Duck	1
Pig	3	Eagle	1
Pigeon	3	Elk	1
Quail	5	Fly	1
Rabbit	2	Fox	
Rat	4	Frog	1
Rooster	2	Grass spirit	1
Rhinoceros	1	Hawk	1
Serpent	3	Hound	1
Shrew	1	Iguana	1
Snake	10	Jay	1
Tiger	7	Mongoose	1
Tortoise	7	Mosquito	1
Tree spirit	10	Mouse	1
Viper	2	Otter	1
Vulture	4	Panther	1
Walter spirit	2	Rhinoceros	1
Wolf	1	Shrew	1
Woodpecker	3	Wolf	1

REFERENCES

1. Padmanabh S. Jaini, "Indian Perspectives on the Spirituality of Animals" in Buddhist Philosophy and Culture, Essays in Honour of N.A., Jayawickrema, ed. David J. Kalupahana and W.G. Weeraratne

(Colombo, Sri Lanka : N.A. Jayawickrema Felicitation volume committee, 1987), p. 169-178.
2. SBE. XIII, 298-99.
3. Vin. I. 64-66. (PTS)
4. Thomas Berry, The Dream of the Earth (San Frassisco : Sieerra Club Books, 1988), p. 11.
5. J. IV. 68-69.
6. J. V. 115-117.
7. Vin. III. 3-4, (PTS)
8. Ibid. p. 1.
9. Sn. X. Verse, 151, p. 24-25.
10. Eugene Walson Burlingame, "Buddhisst Legends," Part I, p. 178.
11. SBE. XX. 247-50.
12. M. II. 54-57 (PTS).
13. A. I. 143-44, (PTS).
14. J. II. 288-89.
15. A. II. 72-73. Also in Vin. II, 110.
16. A. III. 301.
17. A. III. 169.
18. Vin. IV. 32.
19. Ibid. 34.
20. Ibid. 124.
21. Ibid. 125.
22. Ibid. 49.
23. Vin. I. 218-220.

Chapter-2

BUDDHIST CONCEPT OF NON-VIOLENCE (*AHIṂSĀ*) AND ANIMAL PROTECTION

The dearest thing to a human being is his ownself. Any object intimately associated with oneself becomes an object of love for him. As objects of love is treated with tenderness. A man takes care of his body and his family, desiring no violence to himself and his dear ones. This self love culminates into love for all in the case of a broad minded person with a true vision. As a matter of fact, the same self appears in different forms. In the *Gītā*, Lord Krişṇa tells Arjuna that he who sees Him everywhere and all in him, He is not lost to that devotee nor that is lost to the Lord.[1] The essence of the Lord's teaching is that he who is one with all becomes one with the devine.

Ahiṃsā is mainly defined as the absence of *hiṃsā* whereas *hiṃsā* means hurting or injuring[2] others. So, *ahiṃsā* would mean not hurting or injuring others in thought, word or deed. It is of three types (i) *Mānaśīka* i.e. *ahiṃsā* in thought, (ii) *Vācikā* i.e. *ahiṃsā* in word and (iii) *Kāyīkā* i.e. *ahiṃsā* in deed.

Ahiṃsā has got two aspects which are the negative aspect and the positive aspect. Not to injure others is the negative aspect of *ahiṃsā*. Other forms of negative *ahiṃsā* are not to speak harsh words, not to have ill-will, anger, spite, cruelty, not to torture human beings and non-human beings, no starvation, exploitation, humiliation and oppression of the weak, not hurting their self-respect etc. The essence of *hiṃsā* consists in violent desire for *hiṃsā*.

The positive aspect of *ahiṃsā* is the cultivation of goodwill and love towards all. Love implies compassion *(karuṇā)*, forgiveness (*Kṣamā*) and disinterested service (*Sevā*). A person who is non-violent in the positive sense, is compassionate towards the distressed and attempts to put an end to their distress. He loves those who consider themselves to be his enemy and forgives those who do wrong to him. That person thinks that it is his duty to help those who require help. Positive *ahiṃsā* expects of us not to harbour any ill-will because it is well known that evil cannot be overcome by evil, by violence or tit for tat mentality. It can be conquered only through good acts. *Ahiṃsā* in its true sense means to have belief in the essential goodness of human nature. It aims at the realization by the evil of the spiritual oneness with the so called opponent. Absolute positive *ahiṃsā* means to have selfless love for all whether friend or foe. It requires a person to eschew all violence in thought, word and deed. Positive *ahiṃsā* requires fearlessness and innate strength. But it does not mean to oppress the weak and the downtrodden. Fearlessness is an essential quality of a of a non-violent person, which means not to be afraid of hunger, thirst or consequences after having taken the right step, not to be afraid even of death.

Ahiṃsā in the Indian context is defined in two ways, which are :

(i) Etymological meaning as physical non-injury, and

(ii) The popular meaning as non-killing.

It is often wrongly assumed that the etymological meaning of *ahiṃsā* is non-killing or non-injury. In the *Rigveda*, Indra is invoked so that the chanting of *mantras* may not be harmful to the god Indra himself.[3] So, from etymological point of view we can say that *ahiṃsā* is not "non-killing" but physical non-injury in true sense as depicted in the *Rigveda*. In *Taittiriya Samhitā*, the term *ahiṃsā* is used in the sense of non-injury to the sacrificer himself.[4] In *Satapatha Brahmana*, *ahiṃsā* is described as "the womb does not injure the child and the womb remains uninjured (*ahiṃsā*)".[5] T.W. Rhys Davids claims that the word *ahiṃsā* is used for the first time in *Chhandogya Upaniṣad* which must have been documented in the 7th century B.C. But the first reference of *ahiṃsā* in a moral sense may be found in *Kapiśṭhalā-kathā Samhitā* where non-killing of animals is referred to in the context of sacrifice.[6]

But the meaning of the term *ahiṃsā* in the popular sense of "non-killing" is given by *Manu.* If one say that the popular meaning of *hiṃsā* is 'killing' then is quite rightly said that the popular meaning of *ahimsa* is 'non-killing' of a living being. It appears that in the *Dharmaśāstras* and the *Purāṇas,* the word *hiṃsa* is more often used in the sense of 'killing' than *ahiṃsā* in the sense of 'non-killing'. Therefore, the relative frequency of *hiṃsā* in the sense of killing does not establish that *ahiṃsā* is equally often used in the popular sense of non-killing.

The ethical treatment that deliberate harming and hurting of living things should be avoided in private conduct and excluded from public policy is given an important emphasis in Buddhist teachings. However, this particular emphasis is by no means peculiar to Buddhism itself because the *Concept of ahiṃsā* or the Doctrine of Non-violence originated much before the origin of Buddhism itself. The scholars get puzzled when they try to know about its origin. Most of the scholars have been surprisingly elusive on this issue. To know clearly about its origin we will have to go through some detailed discussion.

Non-violence or *Ahiṃsā* and universal compassion such as are epitomised in the word *ahiṃsā* were not by any means discernible emphases in the earliest religious writings of our country, the Vedas. The Vedic gods like Indra on the contrary were portrayed as veritable patrons of war, given to the practice of violence in battel.[7] Besides, the killing of animals in particular for sacrificial purposes was very much a part of early Brahmanical religious ritualism.[8] However, the maturing of the Hindu spirit led to a tracit recognition of ethical primacy and religious value of non-violence. Thus, the *Upaniṣads* and a whole range of later Vedic Hindu writings contain clear references to *ahiṃsā.*[9] Recent investigators often tend to complain that most of these sources fail to delve deeply into the import of *ahiṃsa* and clarify its rational and range of applications. We also find that non-injury is clearly implied in the *Gītā's* teachings on the subject of unselfishness and doing good to others; so, it seems to reflect the fact that *ahiṃsā* has, indeed, been observed in the basic Hindu value structure, since *ahiṃsā* evidently has no firm roots in the vedic culture.

However, modern scholarly investigations have frequently sought to link the original of *ahiṃsā* to certain socio-cultural circumstances, namely, the widespread sense of revulsion felt throughout Northern India over animal slaughter and blood letting involved in the early Brahmanical sacrificial rituals.[10] But it is very difficult to ascertain which tradition first captured and crystallized the claims of mercy and the case for pity that gained ground in the 6th century B.C. Since Buddhism and Jainism were founded in the 6th century B.C., we are forced to look into this matter by comparing both the religions simultaneously. Keeping this aim in mind, I would like to turn our attention towards the Buddhists focusing on *ahiṃsā*, comparing and contrasting them on occasions to the Jaina positions. "Laying aside violence in respect of all beings, not harming even one of them",[11] was a recurrent theme in Buddhist teachings. And thoughts and sentiments associated with it were woven into these teachings in a complex variety of ways. Needless to say, these thoughts and sentiments have their roots in *ahiṃsā*, the moral requirement that one should desist from injurious conduct.[12] The Buddhist view of special eminence to *ahiṃsā*, however, came to be tersely understood in *Dhammapada* itself subsequently when it was stated that one becomes worthy of being called "noble" (*āriya*) when one renounces harming and harmful practices towards all living beings.[13]

The concept of *ahiṃsā* as it developed in India is closely linked with notions of *Kamma*. In the context of the *Rigveda*, kamma means ritual action. Through one's actions in the sacrificial process, certain benefits are said to be assured. The ethical importance of *kamma* in the Hindu context is found in *Bṛhadaraṇyaka Upaniṣad*, When Yajnavalkaya states that "one becomes good by good action, bad by bad action".[14] It is only in the later *Dharmaśāstra* materials that the specific doctrine of rebirth according to one's meritorious or sinful deeds is fully expounded.[15] Within the very first written documents of the Jaina Tradition by contrast, we see a fully developed and quite distinct doctrine of *Kamma* that entails strict observance of ethical precepts rooted in *ahiṃsā.* The earliest extant text of the Jainas, *Acāranga Sutta,* dating from the 4th century B.C. proclaims a much stronger message than that of Yajñavalkaya. Injurious activities inspired by self-interest lead to evil and darkness. This is what is called bondage, delusion death and hell. To do harm to others is to do harm to oneself.

The Buddha, the enlightened one was an embodiment of mercifulness, compassion, selfless love, forgiveness, truth and purity. He renounced the world to know the truth and after great austerity and penance, realized suffering, its course and the means to uproot this suffering which entraps every creature of this world. Buddhism did not start as a new and independent religion but it was an offshoot of the more ancient faith of the Hindus, perhaps a schism or a heresy. Buddhism originated in India as a religious movement easily distinguishable from Hinduism due to its lack of allegiance to Vedic text and its disdain for animal sacrifices.

Ahiṃsā, translated as non-violence in simple English is an impulse from without tending to force one without any concurrence on its part to act against its choice. The stimulus or moving cause must come from without; no one can do *hiṃsā* to himself. The person compelled to act or to abstain from action not only assists this external force but resists and as far as possible strives against it : if he is merely indifferent, there is no *ahiṃsā. Ahiṃsā* cannot affect the will directly i.e. the elicited acts of the will, since it is contrary to the essential notion of an act to the will that should not be free. Acts however that are merely commanded by the will and exercised through the medium of some other faculty, internal or external, may be coerced, since these faculties may be impeded by *ahiṃsā* from putting into execution on the behests of the will. Since, then, acts commanded by the will may suffer from *ahiṃsā, ahiṃsā* to that extent causes involuntariness and freedom from imputability. It is apparent that insofar as coercion is irresistible, the agent is not responsible for the resulting external act.

Ahiṃsā that is not absolute may be weakened or overcome by resistance. The more vehement it is the more is our freedom limited. He, then, who, can by resisting, repel *ahiṃsā* and does not, at least indirectly, desires to suffer *ahiṃsā. Ahiṃsā* means not injuring anything, harmlessness, security and safeness.[16] The etymological meaning of *ahiṃsā* is not 'non-killing', but 'physical non-injury'[17] leading to pain or suffering. However, in the *Pāli Pañcanikāyas,* the term *avihiṃsā* means "absence of cruelty, mercy, humanity, friendliness & love". According to Unto Tahtinen, in Pāli Buddhist texts many words for *ahiṃsā* are used :

"*Avihiṃsā,* Pāli texts, refers mainly to mental non-violence in the form of intention or resolution (*avihiṃsā-samkappa*) whereas the rule 'not to kill living beings' is expressed by the words *panatipāta veramānī.* Another term for non-hurting is *aviheṭhanā,* the absence of various types of harassments".[18]

He further points out some other Pāli words that should be noticed : *Anūpaghāta* which means non-injury, but more specially absence of less intensive injury; *Anoparambha* which means non-offensive; *daṇḍa* which means a stick, punishment and physical injury; sometimes *daṇḍa* and *duccarita* are synonymous, which means wrong behaviour in body, speech and thought, which afflicts and injures and brings one to trouble and suffering.[19] However, Akira Hirakawa considers the two terms *panatipāta veramāni* and *panatipāta pativirati* used as reference to *śila* and *vinaya* in the rules forbidding the killing of living beings.[20] I.B. Horner and A.K. Commaraswamy call, *ahiṃsā* as the virtue of innocence.[21] In short, the etymological meaning of *ahiṃsā* in Buddhism is quite different from its meaning in other religions because it mainly convey the meaning of spirit and psychology as the mental non-violence in the form of intention. The Buddhist *ahiṃsā* is also found in the Noble Eight-fold Patha (*Āriya-atthāngika magga*), in the fourth item i.e., Right Action (*Samma-kammānta*) that can be explained and interpreted as *ahiṃsā* :

"And what, your reverences, is right action? Refraining from onslaught on creatures, refraining from taking what has not been given, refraining from giving in wrongly to the sense-pleasures..."[22]

It is very obvious that the real meaning of *ahiṃsā* is mental non-anger (*avera*), non-injury (*avihiṃsā*), non-harsh (*akakkasa*), non-ill will (*abyapajja*) to regulate our attitude to life living the middle path (*Majjhima-patipadā*). Concerning this point of view, Vijitha Rajapakṣe says :

"I propose now to turn to the Buddhists' focus on *ahiṃsā*, comparing and contracting it with the Jaina positions, for Buddhist thinking in this area, it is well to reiterate, avoided many of the extreme commitments of the Jaina".[23]

Thus, violence is violation of human nature or natural man. However, we attempt to reduce it to or consider it as moral approval.[24] *Ahiṃsā* has to be practised by human beings to realize the truth. So, Buddhism has usually exalted *ahiṃsā* but have never been against violence which can not be purified and significant that leads human beings to avoid *hiṃsā*, volitional action, *kamma* which really makes the agent suffer. The Buddha unequivocally proclaimed five ways leading to *hiṃsā* as *Upāli Sutta* records :

"The action goes and fetches living beings. The being is being fetched and experiences pain. The action leads to kill the being. The creature is being killed. After having killed, meat is eaten".[25]

The quotation cited above gives the process of the mind leading (*cetana*) to demerit (*apunna*) and finally to *hiṃsā*. Thus, *hiṃsā* brings evil and bad life which man should overcome or uproot.

According in Unto Tahtinen, *ahiṃsā* as a concept developed in the later Vedic age when animals were sacrificed in worship for pleasing gods.[26] Christopher Key Chapple considers that *ahiṃsā* appeared in the Indus Valley as Jainism developed as a religious practice.[27] However, Vijitha Rajapakṣe is of the opinion that "the maturing of the Hindu spirit led to a tacit recognition of ethical primacy and religious value of non-violence... and that it has no roots in Vedic Culture".[28] He adds :

"These, in short, are the principal questions that I propose to address myself to in what follows. It would be well to reiterate that though both Hinduism and Jainism are drawn into our considerations, the main purpose of this brief inquiry is to highlight and examine the *ahiṃsā* doctrine as developed in early Buddhism from a comparativist's perspective".[29]

Needless to say, whether Buddhism was influenced by other faiths or not, *ahiṃsā* has provided a very unique flavour of its own. One cannot find in any of the recorded Buddha's teachings approval to kill or to fight others. In *Sutta Nipāta*, the Buddha says :

"They praised charity, morality, integrity, amiability, penance, gentleness, non-violence and forbearance".[30]

"Then the gods, the ancestors,

Indra, the titans and

demons cried out as the

sword fell on the cows :

'This is unjust"'[31]

In Buddhism, *ahiṃās* is the presence of mind to prevent unwholesome actions taking place in others. So, *hiṃsā* must be, according to Buddhism, expelled from the mind and heart (*citta or cittekaggata*) by each of us.

Here, I would like to focus on the origin of the Buddhist doctrine of *ahiṃsā*. It is said that the Buddhist concept of *ahiṃsā* has been directly associated with the so called agricultural revolution.[32] This is only an illusion. The idea of economic utility of animals being partly responsible for the unpopularity of sacrifices, was propounded by I.B. Horner way back in the 1940s. She had proposed that the growing realization that large scale sacrifices were both spiritually and economically unsound must have played a decisive part in stamping it out".[33] According to R.S. Sharma, "The Buddhist rejection of animal sacrifices and emphasis on non-injury to animals assumed a new significance in the context of he needs of the new agriculture". In sharp contrast to the Vedic texts, the Buddha asserts that animal sacrifice does not produce any merit. He pointedly and specifically attacks Vedic sacrifices in which animals were killed. Though there may have been some truth in Ms. Horner's argument, but the relationship between economic utility and sacrificial fertility have been blown out of proportion. It seems that the basic and logical reason behind the propagation of non-violence by the Buddha was compassion, sympathy, equanimity, forbearance and good will, which are generally admired and taken as of great fruit and profit by ancient Indian Buddhism."[34] The Buddha asked everyone to "cultivate a boundless (friendly) mind towards all beings",[35] and not only the agricultural ones. If the Buddha had been really concerned about the sudden need of agricultural animals, he would have certainly included the names of these animals in the list of animals whose meat had been declared uneatable by him. We must bear in mind that none of these animals had any fruitful bearing on agriculture and the loss of their lives would have made no difference to agriculture whatsoever. In fact, the Buddha considered agricultural activities as entailing violence because they led to destruction of life.[36] The reason as to why the Buddha criticized animal sacrifices was that they were cruel, illogical and futile.

Moreover, the cow which most importantly contributed towards agriculture, had been protected much earlier, especially the milk-cow. In *Sutta Nipāta* we are told of "brahmanas of old" as having regarded cows as their parents, brothers and kin, as their best friends and as the source of all healthful things, hence in gratitude they never killed cows.[37] Also the evidence provided by ancient Indian Buddhist literature for the suppression of great animal sacrifices suggests that outside brahmanical circles also this practice was not particularly cherished by ordinary people.[38] It must also be remembered that India has won fair amount of notoriety for having too many animals, most of whom are dry and old cows, bulls and which are not only a menace to agriculture in the countryside, but also pose a threat to traffic in the cities. In the days of the Buddha the population of such stray and useless animals might have been no less. The hypothesis may further suffer if we look at the sort of animals which were sacrificed as well as the frequency and the number of animals involved in these sacrifices. Where the common masses in a position to sacrifice animals at will? And did have been popular amongst large chunks of the Gangā valley people? Of all the animals sacrificed, how many agricultural animals were really sacrificed? If we answer these questions, in all probability, we shall never indulge in the fantasy of associating the Buddha's call to stop animal sacrifices with the non-existent agricultural revolution. Moreover, finding an association between two existing realities, may itself be full of dangers. For example, we cannot go by the logic that "since society today needs a lowering of the birth rate and celibacy would contribute to the lowering of it therefore the practice of celibacy in the monastic orders of the country reflects the economic needs of the time".[39] We know this is not so.

Non-violence and universal compassion such as are epitomised in the word *ahiṃsā* were not by any means discussible emphases in the earliest religious writings of India, the Vedas. Vedic gods like Indra, on the contrary, were portrayed as veritable patrons of war, given to the practice of violence in battle.[40] Besides, the killing of animals in particular for sacrificial purpose was very much a part of early Brahmanical religious ritualism. However, the maturing of Hindu spirit led to a tacit recognition of ethical primacy and religious value of non-violence. Thus, the *Upaniṣads* and a whole range of other later Vedic Hindu writings contain clear references of *ahiṃsā*.[41] Since *ahiṃsa* evidently has no firm roots in Vedic culture, one may fairly ask : when, how and why did the emphasis on non-injury or *ahiṃsā* come into being? Who were its original proponents and supporters? Though the position and estimation of *ahiṃsā* and the repudiation of *hiṃsā* deserve to be considered as a uniquely important development in the history of ideas, nothing precisely is known about its genesis. Indeed I.B. Horner has rightly remarked :

"The emergence in India of the notion of *ahiṃsā*, non-harming or non-injury, is historically speaking not clear. Its origin cannot be attributed to a definite date or any particular teacher, social reformer or law giver. The problem of the birth of the idea of non-injury is indeed as obscure as that of 'leaving the world' or forsaking home for homelessness".[42]

There is a little bit of doubt as to which traditions first captured and empathised the claims of mercy and the case for pity that gained ground in the 6th century B.C. These are traceable to the Buddha and Mahavira of early Buddhism and Jainism respectively. I now propose to turn to the Buddhist focus on *ahiṃsā*.

"Laying aside violence in respect of all beings, not harming even one of them".[43] This was the recurrent theme in Buddhist teachings. The Buddhist view of the special eminence of *ahiṃsā*, however, came to be tersely underscored in *Dhammapada* itself subsequently when it was stated that one becomes worthy of being called 'noble' (*ārya*) when one renounces harming and practices "harmlessness towards all living beings".[44] In any event, the practice of projecting *ahiṃsā* as a basic moral value and identifying it as a virtue among other virtues is evident in *Digha Nikāya* elaborations on "moralities" in the section on *śīla* in the *Brahmajāla Sutta.*[45]

The Buddhist literature in particular incorporates a striking array of comments, observations and moral reflections on animals, and all of them are inspired by the view that non-human life forms on earth have an inalienable right to exist and without possessing value such as is independent of human considerations, be they economic or utilitarian. Buddhism's sensitivity to the concerns of animals found classic expression through a systematic and reasoned opposition to the sacrificial slaughter of living beings. Indeed, not only did Buddhism highlight the "injustice" inherent in depriving defenceless creatures of their lives,[46] but also questioned the spiritual efficacy and religious value of sacrificial rites (*yajña*) in the course of which "cows are slaughtered, goats and sheep are slaughtered, poultry and pigs are slaughtered and diverse living creatures come to destruction.[47]

Buddhist humanitarianism rooted in *ahiṃsā* was likewise opposed to infliction of wanton cruelty and furthermore condemned hunting, killing and tracking down of animals for personal use or gain.[48] And last but not least, it is necessary to remember that Buddhist spirituality acknowledges rural applications especially religious and meditational for these sentiments of kindly considerations and universal compassion. Their diffusion was a preferred exercise in Buddhist meditational practice known as *Mettā-Bhāvanā*. It required to pervade "the whole world everywhere, in every way, with a mind of friendliness that is far-reaching, widespread, immeasurable, without enmity and without malevolence".[49] Spiritual fulfilment, peace and happiness are sometimes identified as the fruits of the cultivation of kindness in the true spirit of Buddhism.[50] But it is evident from certain *Milinda Pañhā* and *Visuddhimmagga* celebrations that it was also held to bring in its train a variety of other benefits, many of which touched ordinary life.[51]

The non-killing (*ahiṃsā*) or harmlessness to living beings is the first precept in Buddhism.[52] This precept is based upon the principle of mutual attraction and righteousness common to all nature. To wilfully take life means to disrupt and destroy the inherent wholeness and to blunt feelings of reverence and compassion that form the basis of humaneness. The first precept of not killing is really a call to life and creation even as it is a condemnation of death and destruction. Deliberately to shoot, knife, strangle, drown, crush, poison, burn, electrocute or otherwise inflict pain on a human being or an animal—these are not the only ways to defile this precept. To cause another to kill, torture, or harm any living being likewise offends against the first precept. Thus, to put the flesh of an animal into one's belly makes one an accessory after the fact of its slaughter, simply because if cows, sheep, fowl, and fish, to mention the most common, were not eaten, they would not be killed. With the exception of butchers, hunters and fishermen, who kill for the food they eat, the majority of flesh eaters are only indirectly responsible for the violence and destruction of animals. This, however, does not make them less answerable to the first precept. In modern times, many voices proclaim the sanctity of human life. Many countries have put a ban on death sentence. Schools and police organizations are advised not to inflict corporeal punishment. Human life should, of course, be valued highly, but at the same time the lives of other living beings should be treasured too. Human beings snatch away the lives of other creatures whenever it suits their convenience or purpose. The way of thinking that encourages this behaviour arises from a specifically human brand of violence that defiles the self-evident laws of this universe, opposes the growth of the myriad things in nature and destroys feelings of compassion and reverence arising from our humaneness. In view of such needless destruction of life, it is important that we conscientiously uphold this precept.

Buddhist ethical conduct (*śīla*) is built on a vast conception of universal love and compassion for all living beings on which the teaching of the Buddha is based and non-violence (*ahiṃsā*) is the most important component of *śīla*. *Ahiṃsā* is regarded as a guarantee for the safety of life not only of man, but even of life in various other forms. Though violence (*hiṃsā*) can take place in words, thoughts and deeds, ancient Indian Buddhism was mainly concerned with the last part i.e. violence in deeds in which the destruction of life in various forms takes place.

In the days of the Buddha as well as now, annihilation of life took place broadly in the following four forms :

(i) In the form of sacrifices in which animals life and sometimes human life were destroyed.

(ii) Through the hands of hunters, trappers, butchers, fishermen, etc. for human food and other needs, especially for medicinal purposes. Thus, human consumption of meat and fish entailed an important form of violence.

(iii) Through agriculturing and other related activities like digging, irrigating, ploughing, reaping, trampling on grass and crops, cutting of trees and destruction of *ekindriya jiva* (one-fecultied life) which inhabits plants, trees, soil etc.

(iv) In fighting in an organised way through wars, battles etc. and in an unorganised way through murders etc.

Buddhism makes a distinction between man and animals plus plants, seeds etc. Though destruction of or injury to both involves sin, there is a difference of degree. The sin accrued by killing a man is more than the cutting of a plant.

Buddhism makes a distinction between man and animals plus plants, seeds etc. Though destruction of or injury to both involves sin, there is a difference of degree. The sin accrued by killing a man is more than the cutting of a plant. The sin accrued as a result of killing a person with a developed mind is more than a man whose mind is less developed.

Sacrifice in various forms, especially the ones in which animals were deprived of their life, was seen by the Buddha as not only a ridiculous absurdity but also as unpardonable cruelty. He did not recognise the efficacy of sacrifices on the one hand and highly regarded the life of living beings, on the other. According to him, "all living beings are not to be harmed".[53] The sort of sacrifice... (where)... creatures are put to an end is neither of great fruitfulness nor of great profit; nor of great renown; nor of widespread effect. It is just as if a farmer were to enter a wood taking with him the plough and the seeds, and were there in an untilled tract, in unfavourable soil, among unuprooted stumps, to plant seeds that were broken, rotten, spoilt by wind and heat, out of season, not in good condition, and the gods were not to give good rain in due season".[54]

The principle of *ahiṃsā* is held in high esteem in most of the Indian religions. This concept is pre-Buddhist and was used by the authors of the *Upaniṣads*[55] in connection with the cruetly of Vedic *yajñas.* It is from this that the concept of vegetarianism developed. In the fifth century BC, it was strongly advocated by the Buddha, who included it amongst his main teachings and provided it as a theoretical basis. This is regarded as of incomparable merit.

The Buddhist doctrine of *ahiṃsā* is a moderate one and

does not go to extremes. It is often expressed in phrases like *panatipāta veramānī* (abstaining from injuring living creatures) and *panatipāta pativīratī* (restraining oneself from injuring living beings). In Buddhism, non-violence is taught from the standpoint that all people love their own lives and do not wish to be hurt or killed by others. This feeling of self-preservation and self-love is transferred in thought to other people and in this way the love for and protection of life come to be promoted. This is clearly specified in Buddhist texts :

"All tremble before punishment; all fear death. Comparing others with oneself one should not slay, nor cause to slay".[56]

Ahiṃsā is advocated not only from the point of view of compassion and love towards all living beings, it is also maintained from the standpoint of a penitent and a feeling of shame because of the brutality and cruelty involved in killing living beings.

We are told in the *Samāññaphala Sutta* that, "the bhikkhu, putting away the killing of living beings holds aloof from the destruction of life. The cudgel and the sword he has laid aside, and ashamed of roughness, and full of mercy, he dwells compassionate and kind to all creatures that have life".[57]

"Na tenā āriyo hoti, yena panāni hiṃsati,
Ahiṃsā sabbapananam, āriyo'ti pavuccati".[58]

(One does not become noble because one kills living beings,

By non-viollence towards all living beings one becomes noble).

The practice of *ahiṃsā* is not limited to human beings only but includes all living beings. Its basis is compassion (*daya*), mercy (*hitanukampā*) and a feeling of shame (*lajjā*) of the cruelty of killing and injuring life. In this way, *ahiṃsā* has been amalgamated by Buddhism with compassion and a consciousness of shame. Where there is compassion in the heart, it is expressed in an outward act as *ahimṣā*. *Ahiṃsā* is considered a noble act because it is not only the object of the act, but it also results in happiness to the one who practises it. On the other hand, those who harbour hatred, not only injure others but also bring unhappiness to themselves :

"Hatred never ceases by hatred in this world. Through loving kindness it comes to an end. This is an ancient law."[59]

"Who kills not, nor aught causes to be killed,

Who robes not, not makes others rob, for all

Within his heart hath share, he hateth none".[60]

The killing of living beings is a shameful act and is wrong because it opposes the spirit of compassion. Moreover, when *ahiṃsā* is practised one comes to know the true feeling of love and attains happiness. The attainment of this kind of happiness is said to be spiritually of a highly exalted state :

"The sage who injures none
who aye controls himself.
Goes to the everlasting state
where those who go don't grieve".[61]
"Gotamas disciples are always well awake;
Both day and night their minds in harmlessness delight".[62]
With all am I a friend, comrade to all,
And to all creatures kind and merciful;
A heart of amity I cultivate,
And ever in good-will is my delight".[63]

In this way, taking delight in *ahiṃsā* and cultivating a mind of compassion (*mettā-citta-bhāvanā*) are one and the same. Thus, to develop a compassionate heart is to desire happiness and well-being of all living beings. The awakening in oneself of the feeling of compassion towards innumerable and infinite kinds of life, and thus embracing all life by the thought of compassion, is called the mind of boundless compassion (*metta appanañña.* As a result, at this point *ahiṃsā* also fuses with the principle of the mind of boundless compassion.. This principle means that the mind achieves serenity by developing a compassionate heart and thus attains emancipation. Thus, the development of the compassionate heart is something that hoists a man to greater spiritual heights and finally leads him to emancipation.

As a result, the doctrine of *ahiṃsa* is taught in Buddhism in different ways. For instance, *Samma Kammānta* (Right Action) in the Noble Eightfold Path can be demonstrated and expounded as *ahiṃsā*.[64] Similarly, the first step in *Dasakuśalakammapatha* (path of ten kinds of good actions) is that of not killing living beings.[65] In the same way, when the Buddha preached the proper everyday deportment of a lay devotee to Sinugālikā, the first principle pronounced was that of non-killing of beings.[66]

Though *ahiṃsā* is a wonderful act, it is very difficult to practise. Men have invariable passion in them to hit others. Most of the sports and the games that men play are also violence-related one way or the other. Man, in spite of his desire for peace, often stirs up war and strife. More than that, in order to survive, man must eat and most of man's food consists of various kinds of animals. Further, when one is attacked by others, he resorts to killing in self-defence. Then there is the question of various kinds of harmful insects like flies and mosquitoes that have to be eliminated in large numbers in order to minimize the risk of the harmful germs carried by them. Various kinds of drugs also kill harmful germs in the body so that humans can recover from various kinds of ailments. Scientists conduct experiment on animals in order to find cures for diseases that afflict humans. Therefore, the principle of *ahiṃsā* is impossible to uphold literally. In other words, the world in which man lives is a world of mutual injury and life is sustained by sacrificing others. No doubt, the Buddha viewed existence as *dukkha* (suffering).

The practice of perfect and absolute *ahiṃsā* is impossible. "The actual practice of *ahiṃsā* can be undertaken only on the basis of a true cognition of life, the contradictions of which are difficult to resolve".[67] Thus, the inward feeling of the spirit of *ahiṃsā*, and its outward manifestation, the act of *ahiṃsā*, become different from each other. "The action of *ahiṃsā* is difficult to perfect, but the spirit of *ahiṃsā* in the heart is not impossible to perfect by learning. When the inner feeling of *ahiṃsā* becomes complete and perfect it gets expressed in outward actions, and where the two harmonise in actual life it can be called the life of the true follower of the Buddha".[68] As a result, in recognition of the fact that complete *ahiṃsā* is difficult to practise, the Buddha did not formulate strict rules for *ahiṃsā* as action.

A lay follower (*upāsaka*) is exhorted to follow the *Pañcaśila* (Five Precepts) of which the first one is that of non-injury to living beings (*panatipāta vernamānī sikkhāpadam*). As a result, the lay follower undertakes to abstain from injury to living beings not only as a matter of intent but also by actualising it in action. Despite having the intent, when one cannot practise it in real life on certain occasions, the precept is broken. This sort of breach of the precept means that while the intent of *ahiṃsā* is there, the selfish desires opposed to this intent are very strong. In such circumstances, there is inevitably a regret for the breach of the precept and thus, confession (*paṭidesanā*) is made. However, this confession must come from the heart.

The importance of the doctrine of *ahiṃsā* in Buddhism can be measured from the fact that the precept of *ahiṃsa* is included in the *Atthanugikā-uposatha* (Eight Precepts) which is practised by the Buddhists on the four days of *uposaṭha* (fast) of the month. It is also included as the first of the ten precepts for the *samanera* (Bhikkhus) and *samaneri* (Bhikkhunis). The non-killing of life is given in great detail in the *Pātimokkha*, in the *Vinaya* of the bhikkhus and the bhikkhunis. The third precept of the *parājika* in the *Pātimokka* forbids the killing of a human being with intent.

Ordering others to kill, giving advice leading others to commit suicide are also seen as amounting to the same offence as that of murder. Abortion is also placed on the same level as killing a human being. For such an offence, the offending bhikkhu or the bhikkhuni is expelled from the *Saṃgha*, which is the severest punishment for the members of the Saṃgha. When a person is killed accidentally, however, and the intention to kill is not present, the concerned bhikkhu/bhikkhuni is released through confession. Suicide is also forbidden in Buddhism.[69]

According to the Buddha, the perfect person "abstains from injury to seed life and plant life" (*bijagāma bhutagāma*).[70]

He called upon all "to have compassion on creatures".[71] The Buddha felt that the humane sentiment of mankind is not to be limited merely to themselves but should be extended to all sentient beings who should share as much kindness as mankind itself does. The Buddha taught "never to destroy the life of any living creature, however tiny it might be".[72] He, in fact, went on to say that as "everyone fears violence, everyone like life; comparing oneself with others one would never slay or cause to slay".[73] It is forbidden even to throw the remains of food on green grass or into water because the creatures living in both water and grass can be harmed.[74] According to him "making onslaught on creatures, being cruel, bloody-handed, intent on injury and killing, and without mercy on living creatures... is conducive to shortness of life span"[75] and he saw it as repulsive (*cāmāgandha*).[76]

All those following "a bloody calling" like a butcher, fowler, hunter, fisherman, bandit, executioner or a jailor, are seen by Buddhism with a distinct disfavour who get heavy punishments.[77] A cattle-butcher is punished for "many hundred thousands of years in purgatory".[78] Some of the *kāmmic* results which a man brings upon himself by committing injury to a life are "suffering in an unpleasant state for a long period and rebirth in some lower form of being. If born again as man, he may be infirm, ugly, unpopular, cowardly, divested of compassion, subject to disease, dejected and mournful, separated from the company of loved ones, and unable to attain ripe age".[79] The circumstances under which a being is killed as well as the physical and mental development of the being decide the gravity of the moral guilt involved in killing. The *kāmmic* "result of killing a man and killing a child vary in proportion to the physical and mental development of the two".[80] "One never sees or hears of a butcher slaughtering and selling cattle, rams, pigs... or beasts of the forest and living in the abundance of great wealth".[81]

Some of the violent occupations or acts which are recorded in Buddhist literature are as follows :

1. Butcher[82]
2. Follower[83]
3. Hunter[84]
4. Fisherman[85]
5. Bandit[86]
6. Executioner[87]
7. Jailor[88]
8. Cutting[89]
9. Flogging[90]
10. Binding[91]
11. Highway Robbery[92]
12. Plundering[93]
13. Murder[94]
14. Throwing remains of food on green grass or into water.[94]
15. Praising the beauty of death.[95]
16. Inciting someone to commit suicide.[96]
17. To commit suicide.

The prefect One is one who has scruples, is kind and has compassion for every living thing"[97] and "he abstains from cutting, flogging, binding, highway robbery, plundering and deeds of violence".[98] "The one who takes life and further encourages another to do the same... is called the still more unworthy man".[99]

Not even "for the sake of sustaining life would he intentionally deprive any being of life",[100] said the Buddha. Water must be strained before drinking because it contains living things[101] and only that fruit should be eaten which "has not yet any seed in it... (or)... has no more seed in it".[102] Buddhism condemns strongly the one "who should deliberately (*iṭṭamāno*) and purposely (*cittasamkappa*) in various ways praise the beauty of death or should incite (anyone) to death".[103]

In unavoidable circumstances, "indirect killing" was allowed by the Buddha, e.g., "the use of skins, such as sheep-skins, goat-skins and deer-skins as coverlets in all the border countries".[104]

The Buddha said that even for sustaining life animals may not be killed.[105] On the other hand, he is quoted to have said that raw flesh and blood may be used in case of non-human disease.[106] Furthermore, innumerable incidents in the *Jātakas* give a clear parole to the Bodhisattva for indulging in killing. We are told that "in certain ccases a Bodhisattva may destroy life",[107] especially when there is a fault in his horoscope".[108] At one place the Bodhisattva indulges in "killing deer and pig, and eating the flesh broiled",[109] then with others chases a thief and "kicked and cuffed him".[110] We also come across the Bodhisattva supplying meat for a coin.[111] The Bodhisattva suffers no visible punishment for all such deeds. On the contrary, he prospers and attains a better world. Moreover, the difficulty arises when the Bodhisattva is born as a carnivorous animal and has to kill not only for himself but also for his herd and, in fact, in such cases the Bodhisattva specialises in killing and hunting techniques.[112]

The attitude of ancient Indian Buddhism towards "warfare, agriculture and meat-eating was more mixed than was its attitude to blood sacrifices. It made no whole-hearted condemnation of these three practices although they all entail taking of life".[113] Though the bhikkhus were forbidden to have more than a minimum to do with the armies,[114] soldiers were not admitted into monkhood Saṃgha,[115] and no bhikkhu was allowed to dig soil.[116] The Buddhist attitude appears a bit contradictory. At least indirectly, Buddhism appears to glorify war and there are quite a few examples in *Vinaya* and *Sutta Piṭakas* where fighting and martial qualities are praised and emulated. There are several similes which are purely militaristic in nature, their point usually being to encourage bhikkhus to be steadfast in battle and to wage spiritual battles like the armed ones.[117] There are certain *Jātaka* stories in which the Bodhisattva participates in battle "to win crown... raising his battle cry as he dashed into the fight".[118]

Despite the drum of non-killing being sounded through a town,[119] its having been heard by the kings of yore[120] and landlords laying interdiction upon the slaughter of animals,[121] Buddhism touched non-violence only on the fringe and did not make a deep impact upon it in the sense that killing of animals continued in full swing at least till the days of Aśoka.[122] Except perhaps bringing about a decrease in the popularity of great sacrifices, the Buddha appears to have met with negligible success in the other three fields of violence. The main cause of the Buddhist policy of non-violence being a failure was its being riddled with all sorts of contradictions. The following two reasons further limited its impact :[123]

(i) The masses as well as the rulers did not want to give up the ways of ministering to their ambitions, pleasure or livelihood.

(ii) The Buddha was a not temporal ruler, hence, he had no actual power to impose a body of restrictive regulations and penalties on the laity as he had on his monastic followers.

In the *Matakabhatta Jātaka*, the Bodhisattva thinking about killers, expresses a desire : "If only these beings (*satta*) perceived the outcome of sinning, maybe they would stay away from killing".[124] He also uttered the following on this occasion :

"Evam ca satta janeyum 'dukkha' ayam jatisambhavo'

na pano paninam haññe, panaghati hi socatiti".[125]

If people were only aware that the penalty would be a birth unto sorrow, living beings would stop taking life. Sorrow is indeed the killer's lot.[126]

A man who coerces another commits violence, those who exploit and indulge in forced human labour, those who overhold or goad or otherwise torture animals also commit violence. Thus, coercion, arrogance, and cruelty to animals constitute violence. But motive or attitude or wish relating to an action or thought or behaviour also determine behaviour. An action is an act of violence if it causes harm, if the agent wishes to cause it, if the action is not justified in terms of legitimate self-interest, and if one has a prior duty not to cause the harm. Violence means to inflict harm or injury, both mental and otherwise, on all human and non-human forms of life with some evil intentions or motives.

The Buddhist concept of non-violence has two-facets : the negative one which covers injury inspired by compassion, self-restrain, and the desire to alleviate pain; and the positive one which covers non-injury inspired by the same motive, desire and intention. In other words, positive objective considerations justify injury as an expression of non-violence. Thus, the dual concept of nonviolence is realistic. The negative aspect is based on the recognition of the fact that the universe as such is suffered with death and destruction. No one can survive and live in the world without committing one or the other kind of violence. The positive aspect of non-violence partakes of the nature of a moral ideal without which no social, human, or cosmic order can survive. Violence is inescapable in certain critical situations and cannot be eschewed completely and hence in certain situations application of negative aspect of non-violence is unavoidable. One can see certain examples of the application of the negative concept of non-violence, namely injury with a view to alleviating pain to individuals in critical situations such as the ailing dog or the monkey or the snake nuisance in the monastery or violent defence of the honour of women.

The treatment to animals in Buddhism is included in the first Buddhist percept i.e. not to harm or injure living things. In the *Mahāvagga*, the Buddha proclaims—"A bhikkhu (monk) who has received ordination ought not intentionally to destroy the life of any living being down to a worm or an ant".[127] This concern for animal and plant welfare shaped monastic life. In the early days of the Buddhist community, the monks travelled during all the three seasons i.e. the winter, the summer and the rainy season. The public, however, protested that "they crush the green herbs, they hurt vegetable life, they destroy the life of many small living beings", particularly while travelling during the rainy season.[128] Subsequently, the Buddha required that all bhikkhu enter retreats and stop wandering during the rainy season which is called *vassavasa*. This public protest clearly indicates that the practice of *ahiṃsā* had by that time exerted broad influence, sufficient for people to advocate the adoption of this ethics by members of a religious order.

One indicator of the Buddhist commitment to the ethics of not injuring life forms is found in the abundant references to animals in the teachings of both the Buddha and the later Buddhists. For example, in *Jātakamāla*, the didactic tales told by the Buddha drawn from his past lives, he protrays himself as a non-human being. Animals are said to have contributed to his desire for *nibbāna;* seeing animals and humans suffer caused the Buddha to seek enlightenment. In one such story, the future Buddha nureses back to health a goose that had been shot by his cousin Devadatta. In another anecdote, he feels compassion when he sees a tired farmer ploughing the earth, a bird eating a worm dredged up by the plough and the welts inflicted on the back of the ox by the farmer. The weariness of both the beast and the man helped initiate his quest for total awakening.

In the Buddhist tradition of rebirth it is stated that humans can be reborn as animals if they commit heinous deeds, and that animals can be reborn as humans if they act meritoriously. As James P. McDermott has written :

"After the breaking up of the body after death, individuals of comparatively good conduct will be reborn in a relatively satisfactory state of existence (*sugati*), such as the human state. Those of bad conduct and wrong views, on the contrary, are detained to attain a miserable rebirth (*duggati*) as animals or worse. Thus, for example, if they do not end up in hell itself, individuals who creep or slink along in this life, be they bloody-handed hunters, robbers or whatever, are most likely to be reborn in the form of sneaky or creeping creatures—"snakes, scorpions, centipedes, mongoose, cats, mice, owls, or the like".[129]

In the early Buddhist texts, a great care is taken not to harm animals for fear that other members of the offended species might seek retribution,[130] or that one might be reborn as some sort of animal. It is quite often found that animals are depicted as being capable of meritorious behaviour. In one passage from *Vinaya Piṭaka,* an instance of amity among a partridge, a monkey and an elephant is cited as exemplary for Buddhist monks.[131] In *Nigrodhamiggā Jātaka,* a prior incarnation of the Buddha in the form of a deer offers his own life to replace that of a pregnant doe headed for slaughter. The deer's generosity appeals to the reigning king's sense of compassion, who then grants guarantee protection of all deer and ultimately animals, birds and fish in the realm.[132]

Animals have been shown to be receptive to hearing and the teachings of the Buddha. One of the *Jātaka* tales is particularly instructive in regard to the importance of non-injury to living beings. The story goes like this—

Once upon a time, a goat was led to a temple and was about to be sacrificed by the presiding Brahmana. Suddenly, the goat let out a laugh and then uttered a moaninng cry. The Brahmana, startled by his odd behaviour, asked the goat what the matter was. The goat responded, "Sir, first I remembered the history of what has led up to this event. In the last 500 lives I have suffered as a goat and in my next life I will return as a human. The reason I cried is out of compassion for you. You see, 500 births ago I was a Brahman I leading a goat to sacrifice. After killing the goat, I was condemned to 500 lives a goat. If you kill me you will suffer the same fate." The Brahman, visibly shaken, immediately freed the goat who trotted away. A few minutes later, lightening stuck the goat and he was freed to become human again. The Brahman likewise won regard, due to the goats compassionate intervention.[133]

The concern for animal welfare was not confined to the Buddhist monastic community only. Aśoka, the Great king of Magadha, who converted to Buddhism, enacted several laws that required kind treatment of animals. These include restrictions on meat consumption, curtailing hunting and establishing hospitals and roadside watering stations for animals. Exerpts from Aśoka's inscription, translated from rocks and pillars still standing throughout India are as follows :

Formerly in the kitchens of the Beloved of the gods, king Piyadashin (King Aśoka), many hundred thousand of animals were killed every day for the sake of curry. But now when this Dharma-rescript is written, only three animals are being killed (every day) for the sake of curry viz. two peacocks (and) one deer (and), the deer again, not always. Even these three animals shall not be killed in the future.[134]

Everywhere in the dominion of the Beloved of the gods, king Piyadassi (Aśoka) ... everywhere (Provision) has been made by the beloved of the gods, King Piyadassi (for) two (kinds of) medical treatment (viz.) medical treatment for men and animals. And wherever there are no (medicinal) herbs that are suitable for men and animals, everywhere (such) have been caused to be brought and caused to be planted. And wherever there are no (medicinal) roots and fruits, everywhere (such) have been caused to be brought and caused to be planted. And on the roads, well have been caused to be dug and trees have been caused to be planted, for use of animals and men.[135] On bipeds and quadrupeds on birds and aquatic animals various benefits have been conferred by me (even) as far as the grant of life.[136] The beloved of the gods, king Piyadassi (King Aśoka), spoke thus : (when I am) crowned twenty-six years, these various (animals) are declared by me inviolable viz. parrots, mainas, the aruṇa, suddy geese, wild ducks, the nandimukhā, the gelata, bats, the ambakapilika, small tortoise, boneless fish, the vedaveyaka, the ganga puputika, the sankenja fish, large tortoise and porcupines, squirrels, young deer, balls the okapinda, wild asses, white pigeons, village pigeons (and) all quadrupeds which are neither useful nor edible.

Those she-goats, eves and sows (which) are either with young or are giving milk (to their young) are inviolable, and (so) also (are) those (of their) young ones which are less than six months old......

Husks containing living being (i.e. insects) are not be burnt.

Frost are not to be burnt, either uselessly or for killing animals.

One animal is not to be fed with another animal... on every fast day, fish was inviolable and are not be sold... (on specific days) he-goats, rams, boars, and other animals that are usually castrated are not to be castrated... (and) the branding of horses and bullocks is not to done.[137]

Though in many ways a partial assertion of animals' rights these inscriptions nonetheless reveal a highly unusual compassion on the part of a temporal ruler towards his subjects, both human and natural.

The *Dasabhumika Sutta* is an important Buddhist text which states that a Buddhist "must not hate any being and cannot kill a living creature even in thought.[138] Kṣemendra writes" I cannot kill and endure the pain even to an ant.[139] In the *Boddhisattva-bhumi* discussion of giving (*dāna*), the first of the six perfections (*pāramitā*), the Buddhist is not allowed to give anything that "may be used to inflict injury on living beings", nor is allowed to give "poisons, weapons, intoxicating liquors and sets for the capture of animals". A Buddhist must" not bestow upon others a piece of land on which the animals may be hunted or killed.[140]

The sixteenth minor precept in the *Brahmajāla Sutta* of *Dīgha Nikāya*, a Buddhist text, graphically states that "one should be willing to forsake one's entire body, one's flesh, hands and feet as an offering to starving tigers, wolves, lions and hungry ghosts".[141] Although this example is undoubtedly overstated but the message is very clear that the animals are to be treated with great respect.

The twentieth precept of the *Brahmajāla Sutta* declares :

"If one is a son of the Buddha, One must, with a merciful. Heart, intentionally practise the work of liberating living beings."

All men are our fathers, all women are our mothers.

All our existence have taken birth from them.

Therefore, all living beings of the six gati (animals, human, gods, titans, demons, hungry ghosts) are our parents and if we kill them, we will kill our parents and also our former bodies, and all the fire and wind are our original substance. Thus, you must always practise liberation of living beings (since to produce and receive life is the eternal law) and cause others to do so; and if one sees a person killing animals, he must by proper means protect them and free them from their misery and danger.[142]

The tremendous emphasis on *ahiṃsā* is yet another manifestation of the Buddhist attempt to have a humanistic attitude towards animals. The large scale destruction of animal life due to sacrifices and customary habit was a serious threat to the existing equations between human beings and non-human beings. The Buddhist response in the form of non-violence *(ahiṃsā)* emerges as a major instrument of social action.

The Buddha condemned and indicted sacrifices "as the sort of sacrifice ... where ... creatures are put to an end ... is neither of great fruitfulness, nor of great profit, nor of great reknown, nor of widespread effect. It is just as if a farmer were to enter a wood taking with him the plough and the seed, and were there in an untilled tract, in unfavourable soil, among, unuprooted stumps to plant seeds that were broken rotten, spoilt by wind and heat, out of season, not in good condition and the gods were not to give good rain in due season".[143]

The Buddha taught his disciples to have "compassion for all creatures"[144] and "never to destroy the life of any living creature, however tiny it might be."[145] *Karniyamettā Sutta* enjoins the practice of *mettā* (loving kindness) towards all creatures timid and bold, short and long, small and big, minute and great, invisible and visible, near and far awaiting birth and already born.[146] While a cattle butcher is punished for many hundred thousands of years in purgatory"[147] a layperson is expected to abstain from trading in meat.[148] The Buddhist bhikkhus and bhikkhunis are to follows an even stricter code so that living creatures are not harmed even unintentionally. For instance, the Buddha promulgated a rule against going on a journey during the rainy season because of possible injury to worms and insects that come to the surface in that weather.[149] The same concern for non-violence prevents a bhikkhu from digging the ground.[150] Once a bhikkhu who was a potter prior to ordination built for himself a clay hut and set it on fire to give it fine finish but the Buddha strongly objected to this as so many living creatures would have been burnt in the process. The hut was broken down on the instructions of the Buddha to prevent it from creating a precedent for later generations.[151] The scrupulous non-violent attitude towards even the smallest living creatures prevents the bhikkhus from drinking unstrained water. It is no doubt a sound hygienic habit but what is noteworthy is the reason which prompts the practice, namely, sympathy for living creatures.[152]

The *Nandivisāla Jātaka* shows how to behave kindly with domesticated animals.[153] Wild animals can also be tamed with kindness and compassion. Once when the Buddha was away from the bhikkhus, a wild elephant Parilleyayaka attented on the Buddha.[154] Even the mad elephant Nālagīrī was tamed by the Buddha's kind words and compassion shown to him.[155] It shows that man and animals can live in harmony if shows loving kindness towards them.

The Buddhist theory of *Kamma* and Rebirth also prepares an individual to adopt sympathetic attitude towards animals. According to this theory, any man can be reborn in a sub-human state among animals.[156] The Buddhist notion of merit teaches a gentle attitude towards living creatures. According to the *Jātaka* stories "One throws dish-washing water into a pool where there are insects and living creatures, intending that they feed on the tiny particles of food thus washed away, on accumulated merit even by such trivial generosity.[157] Again according to *Macchuddāna Jātaka*, once the Boddhisattva threw his left over food to feed the fish and due to that merit he was saved from a disaster.[158]

To conclude, we can say that *ahiṃsā* is like a lamp that brings its believers and practioners out of the darkness of ignorance and clears and enlightens their intellect and wisdom. A practioner of *ahiṃsā* protects not only himself but other living creatures. According to *Digha Nikāya*, if a human being refrains from taking of life and behaves gently, compassionately, mercifully and friendlity all living creatures' he is reborn after death in a bright and blessed world.

REFERENCES

1. *The Bhāgwat Gitā* VI, p. 30.
2. *Sanskrit English Dictionary* by M. William, p. 1171.
3. *Rigveda* 10.22.13.
4. *Taittiriya Samhitā* 5.2.8.7.
5. *Satapatha Brahmana*-6.3.1.26.
6. *Kapiṣṭhalā-kathā Samhitā*-31.11
7. Cf. T.J. Hopkins, *The Hindu Religious Tradition*, Belmont California 1971, p. 13, See also R.C. Majumdar, The Vedic Age, Bombay 1965.
8. It is useful to observe that as A.A. Macdonnell (A History of Sanskrit Literature, Delhi, 1978, p. 126-27) has indicated, cattle which received respectful considerations in later Hinduism did not escape such sacrificial slaughter. The *Rigveda,* he has noted, "Shows that even the cows was slaughtered on special occasions, while bulls are several times described as sacrificial to Indra in large numbers." Frequently, the horse, however, remained the preferred victim. Horse sacrifice, according to him, "was regarded one of the most important and efficacious of animal sacrifices". Some have conjectured that animals were later substituted for human sacrifice. In any event, it will be shown later that the Pāli canon incorporates some explicit attacks on these hurtful rites and practices.
9. For example see *Chhandogya Upaniṣads* III : 17:4, The Bhāgwata Gitā Y.S; XIII, 7 XVI, 2; XVII, 14; *Mānava-Dharmaśāstra.* II. 177; X. 63; XVIII:14; *Yoga Sāstra,* II : 30, 35.
10. Cf. B.G. Gokhale (op.cit., p. 74)... "non-violence first appears as a reaction to the wanton and widespread slaughter of animals in vedic sacrifices in the 6th century B.C.
11. See the Rhinoceros Horn (Suttanipata from K.R. Norman with alternative translation by I.B. Horner & Ven. W. Rahul) London, 1989, p. 7.
12. I.B. Horner (*Early Buddhism and The Taking of Life*, p. 3)
13. *Dh.* Verse 270.
14. *Yajnavalkya Smṛti*, 3.2.10-13.
15. Christopher Kay Chappe, *Non-violence to Animals, Earth and self in Asian Tradition.*
16. M. Monier Williams (1993), p. 125.
17. Unto Tahtinen, *Ahiṃsā* (1976) (London, Rider and Company), p. 2.
18. Ibid. 1976, p. 10.
19. M. II. 37.
20. *Encyclopaedia of Buddhism*, (1961), p. 287.
21. A.K. Coomaraswamy & I.B. Horner (1982), p. 32.
22. M. III. 298.
23. Vijitha Rajapaksa, *Journal of Buddhist and Pali University of Sri Lanka* (1991), vol. 3, p. 49.

24. Unto Tahtinen, *Ahiṃsā* (991976) (London : Rider & Company), p. 14.
25. M. II. 38-50.
26. Unto Tantinen : 1976, p. 33-34.
27. Christopher K. Chappel, 1995, p. 5-9.
28. V. Rajapakṣe, *The Journal of Buddhist and Pali, University of Sri Lanka*, vol. 3, 1991, p. 48.
29. Ibid.
30. Sn. 33.
31. Sn. 34.
32. See for example, amongst others, R.S. Sharma 96, 1983a.
33. I.B. Horner, '*Early Buddhism and Taking of Life*, D.R. Bhandarkar, K.A. Nilakanth Sastri et.al., (ed.) B.C. Law vol. I. 1945, p. 440.
34. KS. V. 149.
35. SBE. X. 25.
36. Vin. IV. 33.
37. Sn. V. 295-97.
38. I.B. Horner, *Early Buddhism and Taking of Life*, (1945) 442.
39. G.C. Pande : "*On the Question of the Social Origins of Buddhism*" (Motilal Banarasidass, New Delhi), 1984; 6.
40. T.J. Hopkins, *The Hindu Religious Tradition*, Belmont Confernja 1971, p. 13.
41. See for example, *Chandogya Upaniṣad*, III : 17:4; The *Bhāgavad Gitā*, X:5; XIII; 7 : XVI:2:XVII:1114: *Mānava-Dharmaśāstra*, II. 177:X:63; XVII:14; *Yoga Sutra*, II:30, 35.
42. I.B. Horber, *Early Buddhism and the Taking of Life*, p. 3
43. See the Rhinoceros Horn. (*Sutta-Nipāta* translated by K.R. Norman with alternative translation by I.B. Horner and Ven. W. Rahul), London, 1985, p. 7.
44. Verse 270. This verse, it is interesting to note, is attributed to the Buddha himself. Its origins are traced to an attempt to pursuade a fisherman to give up his hurtful calling Nārada Thera. The Dhammapada, Introduction, p. IX, Compassion towards animal, always an important component of *ahimsā* tends to come to the fore directly in several other Buddhist works in similar vein. See for example, *Udana* chap. I. sec. III, note p. 39.
45. T.W. Rhys Davids, *Dialogues of Buddha*, London, 1977, Part I. p. 3-4.
46. See the Rhinoceros Horn (*Sutta-Nipāta*), p. 50-51.
47. GS. II. 49.
48. Dh. verse 270.
49. M. II. 16. Also see p. 336. *Theragāthā*. 244.
50. Dh. verse 368.
51. Milinda's question, translated by I.B. Horner, London 1969, Vol. I. p. 286. *The Path of Purification* p. 337, Both these contents give eleven advantages that stem from the cultivation of loving kindness towards

all living creatures. Among these are peace, freedom from fear, friendship and protection from harm.

52. The other seven precepts being : 1. not to take what is not given; 2. not to engage in improper sexuality; 3. not to tell a lie; 4. not to cause others to use liquors or drugs that confuse or weaken the mind nor to do so oneself; 5. not to speak of the shortcomings of others; 6. not to praise oneself and condemn others; 7. not to revile the three treasures (the Buddha, the Dhamma, and the Saṃgha).
53. GS. II. 183.
54. DB. II. 307f.
55. *Chhandoogya Upaniṣad*. III. 17.
56. Dh. 129.
57. DB. I. 79.
58. Dh. V. 275.
59. Dh. 5.
60. GS. IV. 104.
61. Dh. 225.
62. Dh. 300.
63. Tha. 648.
64. M. III. 251.
65. D.III. 269.
66. D.III. 181.
67. DB. I. 289.
68. DB. I. 289.
69. Vin. III. 73. 82.
70. GS. II. 222.
71. Sn. V. 241.
72. SBE. XXVII. 30; XX. 128.
73. Dh. V. 130.
74. SBE. XVII. 22.
75. M. III. 250.
76. SBE. X. 39.
77. KS. II. 171.
78. KS. II. 170.
79. H. Sadhatissa; 1970:89.
80. *Ibid*. 1970:88.
81. GS. III. 273.
82. KS. II. 171.
83. KS. II. 171.
84. KS. II. 171.
85. KS. II. 171.
86. KS. II. 171.
87. KS. II. 171.
88. KS. II. 171.

89. GS. II. 223.
90. GS. II. 223.
91. GS. II. 223.
92. GS. II. 223.
93. GS. II. 223.
94. SBE. SVII. 22.
95. BD. I. 126.
96. BD. I. 126.
97. GS. II. 221.
98. GS. II. 221.
99. GSs. II. 223.
100. GS. II. 231.
101. GS. IV. 129.
102. BD. III. 3; J.I. 83.
102. SBE. XX. 75.
103. BD. I. 126.
104. SBE. XVII. 39.
105. GS. IV. 129.
106. SBE. II. 43.
107. J. III. 296.
108. J. II. 265.
109. J. IV. 272.
110. J. I. 219.
111. J. I. 295.
112. The *Jātakas* are full of such incidents. The Bodhisattva is born 8 times as a lion and thrice as a vulture.
113. I.B. Horner : *Early Buddhism and Taking of Life*, D.R. Bhandarkar, K.A. Nilakantha Sastri et.al. (eds.) BC. Law, Vol. I. Calcutta, 1945; 443.
114. Vin. IV. 104-108.
115. SBE. XIII. 196, 230.
116. Vin. IV. 33.
117. See, for example, A.II. 116; III.89. 100, 161; J. II. 276.
118. J. I. 205-206.
119. J. III. 428, 434.
120. J. III. 428.
121. J. IV. 115.
122. I.B. Horner : 1945 : 348
123. I.B. Horner : 1945 : 439.
124. J. I. 168.
125. J. I. 168.
126. J. I. 168.
127. *Mahāvagga* 1.78. 4, in *Vinaya Texts*, translated from Pāli by T.W. Rhys Davids and Hermann Oldenberg (Delhi, Motilal Banarasidass, 1974; first published at Oxford University Press, 1882).

128. *Mahāvagga* in *Vinaya Texts,* III. 1.1.
129. James P. McDermott, *"Animals and Humans in Early Buddhism." Indo-Iranian Journal"* (Vol. 3, No. 2, 1989), p. 269.
130. Ibid., p. 274.
131. Ibid., p. 270.
132. Padmanabh & Jain : *"Indian Perspectives on the spirituality of Animals,* op.cit., p. 171.
133. Jātaka Tale 18, retold from H.T. Francis and E.J. Thomas, *Jātaka Tales* (Cambridge University, press, 1916), p. 20-22.
134. Rock Edict I was translated in *Ashoka's Edicts* by Amulya Chandra (Caclutta, The Insitute of Indology, 1956), p. 6.
135. "Rock Edict II" Ashoka's Edicts, p. 66.
136. "Pillar Edict II" Ashoka's Edicts, p. 140.
137. "Pillar Edict V" Ashoka's Edicts, p. 154-56.
138. Har Dayal, *"The Bodhisattva Doctrine in Buddhist Sanskrit Literature,* (London : Keagen Paul 1931), p. 197.
139. Dayal, op.cit., p. 199.
140. Dayal, op.cit., p. 175.
141. The Buddha speaks the *Brahmajāla Sutta* translated by Buddhist Text Translation Society, Dharma Realm Buddhist Univ.), Talmage, California : Buddhist Text Translation Society (1980), p. 150.
142. M.W. de Visser, *Ancient Buddhism in Japan : Sutras and Ceremonies in use in the seventh and eight century A.D. and their History in later times* (Leiden : E.J. Brill, 1935), p. 198.
143. D. II. 370.
144. S. V. 241.
145. Vin. IV, 125.
146. S. IV. 302,
147. Ibid. II. 170.
148. A. III. 208.
149. Vin. I. 137.
150. Ibid. IV, 125.
151. Ibid. III. 42.
152. Ibid. IV, 125.
153. J. I. 191.
154. Dh. I. 58.
155. Vin. II. 194.
156. M. I. 137.
157. A. I. 161.
158. J. II. 423.

Chapter-3

EARLY BUDDHIST ATTIDUE TOWARDS MEAT EATING AND ANIMAL SACRIFICE

It is often seen as surprising that vegetarianism is not more widespread among Buddhists than it is given in Buddhist teachings. In fact, the Buddha's emphasis was on avoidance of killing. So, it is worse to swat a fly–an immediate act of killing–than to eat the carcase of an already dead animal. At the time of the Buddha, vegetarianism was practised by the Jainas, though Jainas see the vegetables eaten by them as containing a life-principle or soul (Jiva). On one occasion, Jainas accused the Buddha of knowingly eating an animal that had been specifically killed for him. The donor denied this and the Buddha explained that a bhikkhu might eat meat provided it was pure in three respects : if the bhikkhu had not seen, suspected or heard that the animal had been killed specifically for him.[1] This means that if a bhikkhu has suspicions because of his having seen or head of the donor hunting, fishing or slaughtering an animal recently, he should ask about the meat and can eat it only if the being was not killed in order to feed him.[2] The Buddha also explains that a bhikkhu receives food as a gift from a donor and his loving kindness for donors and other creatures is not compromised by such eating, if it is 'blameless' by being pure in these three respects.[3] He goes on to empahsize that a donor generates much bad *kamma* by killing a being so as to give alms to himself or to a bhikkhu, through : (i) giving the order to fetch the animal, (ii) its pain and distress as it is dragged with a rope around its neck, (ii) giving the order to kill the animal, (iv) its pain and distress while being killed and (v) the offering of meat to a bhikkhu if it is of a type not permissable for a bhikkhu.

In this chapter, I am going to through high primarily on the following issues : (i) Can the first precept be fairly construed to prohibit meat eating ? If the statements of the Pāli texts, which are presumed to be record of the words of the Buddha, are accepted at face value, it can be argued that the Buddha allowed the eating of animal flesh. But are these portions a later interpolation in Pāli literature ? The view of meat eating is sharply criticized and contradicted by the *Mahāyāna Suttas,* also purporting to be the spoken words of the Buddha, which categorically assert that meat eating is contrary to the spirit and intent of the first precept since it makes one an accessory to the slaying of animals and therefore contravenes the compassionate concern for all life that lies at the core of Buddhism. I have tried to establish in the work that the Buddha could not have uttered the words attributed to him in Pāli literature with regard to meat eating.

(ii) Is there reliable evidence that the Buddha sanctioned meat eating ? Unfortunately no serious attempt has been made by scholars to resolve the glaring discrepancy between the contentions of the two branches of Buddhism on meat eating.

(iii) Following from the previous point, did the Buddha die of eating a piece of pork as claimed by some scholars, or from a poisonous mushroom as asserted by others ? I have tried to establish that the Buddha died as a result of eating a poisonous mushroom and not pork. Surprisingly the Buddha does not put a ban on flesh-eating. A bhikkhu is allowed to accept "what has been put in his alms bowl."[4] In fact, Devadatta, the Buddha's cousin, tried to corner the latter regarding meat-eating when he asked him for a total ban on meat-eating. The Buddha refused to do so even at the cost of losing some of his followers.[5] Devadatta may have been inspired by total prohibition observed by some *samanas* and brahmanas.[6]

Many other references prove, though almost incidentally, that the eating of meat was thought of a customary and bhikkhus are recorded to have eaten flesh and fish frequently enough to give it the appearance of its having been a fairly important part of their diet. Meat, fish, fruit, dairy products and cereals especially rice, constituted the staple food of the population, and the Buddha was strongly convinced that purity did not depend upon food[7] but on restraint over such bodily, mental and moral conduct as could defile a man.[8]

The Buddha allowed bhikkhus to eat meat with the following exceptions:

1. In three cases meat may not be eaten by a bhikkhu if he has (a) seen, (b) heard or (c) suspected that the meat has been especially acquired for him by killing an animal i.e. the animal has been killed on purpose for the bhikkhu.[9] This rule is called *The Rule of Tikotiparisuddha (The Rule of Being Pure in Three Ways)*. Thus, the Buddha did not see any sin being committed by himself or by one of his bhikkhus if the meat had been acquired by some body through deliberately killing an animals to feed it to them.

"The wicked may for gift slay wife or son,

Yet, if the holy eat, no sin is done."[10]

2. Use of raw meat was not allowed.[11] But in case of sickness even raw flesh and blood could be used.[12] "The cooking and eating of the remains of the killed lions, tigers, hyenas and wolves are allowed by the Buddha to be eaten by the bhikkhus.[13] The Buddha also allowed "the use of the fat of bears, fish, alligators, swine, asses, if received at the right time to be partaken of with oil."[14] Indeed, fish and meat are mentioned among the five superior and delicate foods (*panitābhojaniya*) which a bhikkhu who is ill is allowed to eat.[15]

3. The meat of the following ten beings is forbidden to be eaten by the bhikkhus due to variety of reasons involved in their eating[16]:

1. Man
2. Elephant
3. Horse
4. Dog

5. Snake
6. Lion
7. Tiger
8. Leopard
9. Bear
10. Hyena

The *Rule of Tikotiparisuddha* restrained the bhikkhus from being instrumental in killing animals for meat and to a small extent the "rules prohibiting the eating of meat of socially disapproved beings made up for the limitations,"[17] the early Indian Buddhist attitude towards meat-eating and non-violence appears to be somewhat contradictory. The *Rule of Tikotiparisuddha* may have absolved the bhikkhus of any sin, but the slaughter was very severely criticised by them.

Did the Buddha Die of Meat-Eating?

Now the question arises whether the Buddha died of meat-eating? Let us presume that the Buddha would have frequently eaten 'blàmeless' meat given as alms. Thus, the debate over whether his last meal, literally 'pig-mild' (*Sukara-maddava)*,[18] was pork, or truffles dug up by pigs, is rather beside the point. It is notable that the Buddha actually resisted an attempt to make vegetarianism compulsory for bhikkhus.[19] This was proposed by his cousin, Devadatta. In order to foment a schism, he proposed to the Buddha that all bhikkhus should both be vegetarians and follow a number of previously optional ascetic practices, such as living at the root of a tree. The Buddha outrighly rejected it reaffirming that the practices were optional and meat outrightly rejected it reaffirming that the practices were optional and meat was acceptable if it was 'pure in three respects'.

That is why there is a controversy regarding meat eating by the Buddhist bhikkhus among the scholars. The justification of meat eating comes not only from the fact that there are certain instances of the Buddha allowing the eating of meat, the bhikkhus also invariably point out that the Buddha, in fact, had died as a result of eating pork (which was putrid and it poisoned the Buddha) at the home of one of his followers called Cunda. They further point out that they gratefully accept whatever is put before them, without preference or aversion. Various statements and actions of the Buddha are used to justify the eating of meat, implying that if the Buddha himself ate flesh food when it was offered to him, surely they have warrant to do likewise.

Here I will try to point that what the Buddha died of was not a piece of pork but a poisonous truffle that caused his death. Truffle is a species of mushroom. The relevant portion of *Mahāparinibbāna Suttānta* is as follows :

"Then Cunda addressed the Exalted One and Said, "May the Exalted One do the honour of taking his meal, together with the brethren, at my house tomorrow ?"

And the Exalted One signified by his silence his consent...

Now at the end of the night, Cunda, the worker in metals, made ready in his dwelling place sweet rice and cakes, and a quantity of truffles.[20]

The word *Sukara-maddava* has been translated variously by scholars. One of the scholars named Franke has translated it as "soft (tender) boar's flesh".[21] Odlenberg[22] and Fleet[23] also agree with him. However, another word that is used for pork is *sukaramāṃsa.*[24] T.W. Rhys Davids translated it as "quantity of truffles".[25] Arthur Waley[26] gives four interpretations of *sukara-maddava* which are (i) a pig's soft food (food eaten by a pig), (ii) a pig's delight (a favourite food of a pig), (iii) the soft parts of a pig, and (iv) pig-pounded (food trampled by pigs). K.E. Neumann as quoted by Waley "has shown that in Narahari's *Rajanighantu,* among the names of medical plants, there occurs a whole series of compound words having 'pig' as their first element, like *sukara-kanda* (pig-buld), *sukara-pūdika* (pig's foot), *sukareṣṭa* (sought-out by pigs). On the analogy of the last, Neumann takes *sukaramaddava* to mean 'pig's delight', and assumes that it the name of some kind of truffles... Plant names tend to be local and dialectical. It is quite likely that if such an expression as *sukaramaddava* meant "trufles" in Magadha, in more western and southern centres where Pāli Buddhism came into existence, it might have been entirely unknown and consequently misunderstood".[27] The expression *Sukara-śāli* is used for a kind of wild rice.[26]

Edward Thomas says, "The word, however, is not the obvious *sukaramaṃsā*, pig flesh', which we would expect if this were meant".[29] C.A.F. Rhys Davids points out, "A food-compound of pig-flesh (*sukaramaṃsa*) does occur once in the scriptures, in a *sutta* of a curiously unworthy kind, where a householder, in inviting the Buddha to dine, goes through quite a menu in a restrained detail! *Maddava* is nowhere else associated with meat, and I remain of Rhys Davids' opinion that we have here a dish... of a root, such as truffles, much sought by swine, and which may have been called "pig's joy." Such a root we actually have this the critics did not know in our "pignut",... the little nut-shaped bulbous roots of which, called also "earthnuts," are liked by both pigs and children".[30]

Since Cunda had invited the Buddha to his house, he could not have offered pork to the Buddha as it would have meant violation of the *Tikotiparisuddha*, if one were to accept that the Buddha made this rule. Regarding the meal requirements of the Buddha, the would be donors of meals to the Buddha often consulted Cunda. For example, this is amply clarified by a conversation between Cunda and a brahmana in *Vinaya Piṭaka* : "If I were to prepare, my dear Cunda, rice-milk and honey-lumps (for the bhikkhus), would the reverend Buddha accept it from me?

"Well, my good brahmana, I will ask the Blessed One." And the Venerable Cunda told thing to the Blessed One.

"Well, Cunda, let him prepare (these dishes)."

"Well, my good brahmana, you may prepare (those dishes)".[31]

To say that the Buddha sanctioned meat-eating after having taken care of certain conditions is quite difficult to accept. He who condemned animal sacrifices in the strongest possible language and also the bloody trades of slaughtering, hunting, and trapping, is difficult to imagine to have savoured the flesh of the same animals. "I'm only doing your dirty work," was the response of a butcher to a person who objected to the cruelty of the slaughterhouse, "It's such as you make such as us".[32] Each human being who eats flesh, whether an animal is killed expressly for him or not, is supporting the trade of slaughtering and contributing to the violent deaths of harmless animals. Anyone familiar with the numerous accounts of the Buddha's extraordinary compassion and reverence for living beings, for instance, his insistence that his bhikkhus carry filters to strain the water they drink lest they inadvertently cause the death of any micro-organisms in the water, could not have imagined that the Buddha allowed animal flesh to be eaten. Bhikkhus by virtue of their training, their strength of character and their life purpose are different and stronger than the laity and better able to resist the pleasures of the sense to which ordinary people succumb. It appears that bhikkhus and scribes interpolated the portions relating to meat-eating into the *Theravada* scriptures. For over 300 years the scriptures were transmitted orally and as of now they do contain early and later portions.

The Buddha himself (perhaps) died of eating pork, the flesh of a wild boar, an idea so abhorrent to later Buddhism that the word *sukaramaddava,* (boar-tender), -loin? Was interpreted either as a sauce or as a vegetable eaten by a boar; (some said bamboo sprouts, others said a kind of mushroom) although no sauce or vegetable is known by the name of 'boar-tender'. Compare the Questions of Milinda,[33] and the discussion as to bamboo, mushrooms, or sauce.[34] Boar flesh is common village-meat. Compare what the pigs say in *Jātaka* No. 388, *'maṃsatthaya hi posiyamase'*, "We are flattened for our flesh",[35] and further references below. Still, some plant-names begin with 'boar' and the Buddha ought to have the benefit of doubt.[36]

Elephants' flesh and that of horses may not be eaten in times of famine, but this is because they are parts of the "attributes of royalty", nor that of dogs and snakes, but because such meat is disgusting. Absolutely forbidden at such a time is only the flesh of human beings and of other carnivores.[37]

In regard to hurting sentient beings, Brahmanism holds theoretically that even trees, plants, and grass are kinds of animals. They differ only in being stable (fixed) instead of being mobile; but a long argument which I have cited else where from the Great Epic shows that plants really see, hear, feel, and smell as well as possess the more obvious sense of touch and that, therefore, they are living, conscious beings endowed like other animals.

A century after the death, the Buddhist church discussed the question whether it was permissible to drink unfermented toddy. The Buddhist was a teetotaller, as was (ordinarily) the brahman priest, but in this regard, the *saṃgha* as a whole appears to have been much stricter than the orthodox Hindus (not of the priestly caste) who have always been addicted to intoxicants. Even brahman priests, north of the *Nerbuddha,* were rum-drinkers. *Assa nāma rājabhoga,* "horses are king's property".[38] Cannibalism has left its trace in India in the stories of flesh-eating Yakṣas and Piśācas, natives of the Gilgit region.[39]

The Buddhists hold that a tree, for example, is 'conscious' only as containing a living being, a dryad. Plants in themselves possess only one organ of sense, feeling. So there is naturally less horror of injury to plant-life (as plant) among Buddhists than among non-Buddhists (the brahmans and their followers), though rebirth as a plant is more a historical possibility than an actual probability to both parties of believers in *Kamma.* According to a rather late compendium of heresies, the *Brahmajāla Sutta,* the Buddhist recluses, despite the tightening bonds of conventional friarhood, still continued to injure growing plants, though it was wrong to do so, as it was wrong" accept raw meat" and to kill living things. This reveals that raw meat was accepted often enough a make it worthwhile to animadvert upon the practice. But even this *Sutta* (like the rules for novices) does not prohibit the eating of meat.

In the Edicts of Aśoka, there are several injunctions against cruelty, but it is ordered merely that (even of sacrifice) no animals be killed "in future," with a recommendation to respect the sacredness of life. Yet it is evident from the Fifth Pillar Edict of king Aśoka that the killing of animals was not unusual. Certain animals in the twenty-seventh year of Aśoka's reign were made exempted from slaughter, as were "all quadrupeds which are not eaten or otherwise utilized by man," a clear indication that previously the slaughter of animals was not uncommon and that "the more complete abstention from injury to animate creatures and from slaughter of living beings" was, as proclaimed in the Seventh Pillar Edict, brought about by Aśoka, a couple of centuries after the Buddha's death.

There is, unfortunately, no common name for the brahmanized horde as there is for the followers of the Buddha. We have sometimes used 'orthodox' for the horde as the brahmans (i.e. the priests) used heterodox (unbelievers) especially for the Buddhists; but the orthodox were anything but a united fold. Though they all called themselves, as against the Buddhist, 'believers' in plants as 'having only one organ.

The Edicts, however, are not for Buddhists alone but for all in the realms and in this particular respect may be aimed against the brahmanic rather than the Buddhistic practices. Nevertheless, as no party distinction is made, it may be presumed that the Buddhists also needed a stricter rule. In connection with the brahmanic practices, it must be noted that beef-eating in the *Mahābhārata*, though common is confined to ceremonial (sacrificial) consumption.

The *Jātakas* contain numerous instances revealing great freedom in respect of flesh-eating. For example, the *Bodhisattva* as *Sakka*, in *Kumbha-Jātaka* (*Jātaka* no. 512), forbids the use of intoxicants, but permits the enjoyment of flesh (*māṃsodanam sappipayasam bhunja*).[40] In *Jātaka* No. 528, the *Bodhisattava* as a mendicant, *mahabodhiparibhajako*,[41] eats the flesh of a bhikkhuey, (*makkatamāṃsam khāditva*), and uses its skin as a robe, though only in order to impart a lesson. In its Sanskritized form, in *Jātakamālā*, this bhikkhuey apears as an illusion (perhaps because of audience, much as the "fatted calf" is discreetly omitted from another parable in India these days) and the *Bodhisattva* merely "removes a skin made by himself" and then wears it after causing the flesh to disappear (*carma'paniya sesam antardhapayam asa: sa tannirmittam vanaracarma bibhrat,* etc.) That the deer was a warrior's natural food is admitted in a causal remark addressed to a priest in *Jātaka* No. 483, *'annam migo brahmana khattiyassa"*[42] but though a king hunts, it was meritorious to renounce the sport and devote oneself to charity. In *Jātaka* No. 504, the king hunts not only deer but also wild boar, *migāssukaradayo khādhitva,* and eats the broiled vension, *angarapakkam migāmāṃsam.*[43] In *Jātaka* No. 315, the Bodhisattva gets a wagon-load of venison as a gift; but he talks the hunter out of his cruel occupation–*luddaka-kamma.* In *Jātaka* No. 12, a king is persuaded to stop killing deer and all other animals. To eat the flesh of a golden peacock, which gives eternal youth and immortality[44] is perhaps too great a temptation to allow of its being cited as an example; yet the peacock was forbidden food either to the Brahman or to the pre-Aśokan Buddhist. *Jātaka* Nos. 451 and 496 reveal that meat-eating was almost a matter of course, even on the part of the Bodhisattva, who in *Jātaka* No. 199 eats beef, *gomāṃsam;* while the forest-ascetic in *Jātaka* No. 496 says, "I eat meat," just as the speaks of eating jujubes, lotus, etc. *(sakam bhisam madhum māṃsam badaramalakāni ca, tani abhatva bhunjāni aṭṭhi me so pariggāho).*[45] In the introduction to *Sulasa Jātaka,* No. 419, we have a scene depicting a pleasure-garden, where thieves and servants indulge in eating fish, flesh and taking intoxicants, *macchamāṃsasurādini,* which shows the vulgar popularity of flesh-food. But in *Jātaka* No. 436, a noble lady of Banāres is fed on ghee, rice, fish, and flesh[46] by the demon who would woo her. In *Jātaka* No. 434, meat is eaten as delicacy. Large bags of leather, *'mahante cammapasibbake'*, to hold money, are referred to in *Jātaka* No. 336. Leather is used to make chariot-harness which is mentioned in *Jātaka* No. 22 and the clothing of mendicant, *cammasatako paribbajako,* in *Jātaka* No. 324. Roasted pig is used to celebrate a marriage-feast (*Jātaka* Nos. 30 and 286) and roasted lizard is recognized as good food (in *Jātaka* No. 333); though it is a fake Buddhist ascetic, *dussilatapaso,* who in *Jātaka* Nos. 138 and 325 is fond of such diet. Crow's meat is sent to the *Bodhisattva* by the king in *Jātaka* No. 214 and in *Jātaka* No. 220, which tells a story (to illustrate a *Jātaka* verse) which implies that a king regularly ate meat (animals might be slaughtered in Banāres any day except on fast-days). *Jātaka* No. 241 even notes the occasion on which, according to tradition, men who had eaten all the meat they could, first began to dry it : *tasmim kila kale vallurakaranam udāpaditi vadanti.*[47] A very good example of the casual, matter-of-course way in which meat-eating is referred to will be found in *Jātaka* No. 106, wherein a young man is advised by his father, the *Bodhisattva,* not to marry, simply because he will have to run errands for his wife, "when she wants to eat fish or meat or has need of ghee or salt or rice, etc."[48] (*yada macchamāṃsadini vā khāditukama bhavissati sappilonatanduladihi va pan assa aṭṭho bhavissati).* Here the worldly fat girl is imagined as eating meat as naturally as salt, etc. The whole matter of meat-eating is epitomized in the verse ascribed to the *Bodhisattva* in *Telovado Jātaka (Jātaka* No. 246) *bhunjamāno pi sappunno na papena upālippati,* that is, according to the context, if one who has divine wisdom eats fish or meat, even when he know it is prepared for him, he does no wrong. The common use of leather, as Prof. Bloomfiled remarks in his paper has been recently exemplified by excavations made in the Northern deserts. Leather nooses are made in *Jātaka* No. 206.[49]

In the exaggerated language of the *Bodhisattva,* one may even eat the flesh of the donor's wife or child. Only the slayer is sinful, not the eater. The comment is : *samāṃsakam bhattam adasi... samano Gotamo janam uddissa-katam māṃsam bhunjati,* "He gave meat-food. Buddha the ascetic knowingly ate meat prepared especially for him." The Buddha here accepts in full the precepts of the *Bodhisattva.* Not even the fact that the eater knows of the circumstances, makes the eater guilty of sin. But he must eat with no evil in the heart, no indulgence of appetite. With the same liberality, which distinguishes the ethics of the Buddha from that of his ascetic rivals, we find the rule that no evil *Kamma* attaches to an act of unintentional wrong-doing as laid down in the *Kuru-dhamma* of *Jātaka* No. 276, *acetanakam kammam na hoti,*[50] the brahmanic rule being that there must be expiation for unintentional as for intentional sin. Devadatta, the Buddha's rival, permitted no eating of flesh (meat); the Buddha permitted it with restricitions as to the spirit in which it was eaten. In other words, early Buddhism was opposed to this form of asceticism as to other austerities which in themselves are valueless. The distinction between killing and eating may seem rather pharisaical, but it existed. To kill an animal, to be a butcher, a fowler, or a fisher, was wrong, and to connive at salughter in order to gratify appetite was also wrong. But when the beast had been killed without prior connivance on the part of the Buddhist, the flesh might be accepted and eaten. The early Buddhist seems to have thought that, as the animal was dead anyway, he might as well make use of it and did not trouble his consscience with questions of 'tainted' offerings. if uncommonly ascetic, he might refuse it as being a delicacy, but not because meat as meat constituted sinful diet. Probably the later accession of brahmanical converts tended to greater strictness of the Buddhist in this regard. Compare the passage (as cited by Mr. Rouse at this place in his translation) from Hardy's Manual." Those who take life are in fault, but not the persons who eat the flesh. My priests (in contrast with those of Devadatta) have permission to eat whatever is customary to eat in any place or country so that it be done without the indulgence of appetite, or evil deisre".[51] The *Cullavagga* on this point, mentions only fish, but the contention is the same. Compare with this *Jātaka* No. 528 *akamakaraniya-smim kuv-idha pāpena lippati.* For the Brahmani rule,[52] compare *Jātaka* No. 506, where the king-snake refuses to eat frogs especially killed for him, with the idea, *"n'esa man nissaya maressatiti" (nā khādati)*, "not for my sake shall he kill".[53]

With St. Paul 'If eating meat my brother do offend I will eat no more meat.' The theory of transmigration had, I imagine, little to do with the matter either with Buddhists or with brahmans, though the Buddha admits that a man may be reborn as an animal, for in speaking of the death of a perfected saint, he couples together, as the fruit of such saintliness, the destruction of "hell and rebirth as an animal." The *Jātakas,* too, recognize man's rebirth as a beast, but these are not of the earliest Buddhistic era, and generally speaking, the primitive Buddhist is reborn as man and, if not, he is more likely to reappear as an unfettered divinity in consequence of virtue than as an animal in consequence of evil. At any rate, man's rebirth as an animal (with a possible cannibalism) is never suggested as a reason why a Buddhist should not eat meat, although the Brahmanic view was that the animal later would eventually take revenge by eating (in another life) the former eater. Yet even here the idea is not that one should abstain from eating flesh through fear of eating a reincarnated relative. To take life, in distinction from eating meat, results in going to hell or in rebirth either as an animal, a ghost, (*pettivisaye*), a demon, (*asupakaye*), or a human being of short life, *alpayukasamvattanikam hoti ti,* said the *bodhisattva.*[54]

One of the knotty questions is how a future Buddha could be born as an animal. Despite his sufficient wisdom *dharmasanjni'pi,* he had acquired "bits of (evil) *Kamma,*" *kammalesans tans tan samasadya,* which reduced him to a beast. The Bodhisattva himself explains rebirth in animal form as due to neglect in a previous life to perform good deeds (*kuśalakammassa akattata*), as he says : *tvam pana kuśalam akatva tiracchanayoniyam nibbatta.*[55] The same question arises in regard to the sins committed to the *Bodhisattva,* such as reverting to sensuality (*Jātaka* no. 251), keeping and knocking down his wife (*Jātaka* No. 199), seducing a girl (*Jātaka* No. 62), or even leading a band of robbers. In the last case the *Jātaka*-maker ascribes such faults rather vaguely "to the stars," *nakkhattadosena* (*Jātaka* No. 279), apparently forgetful of the Bodhisattva's own words, *kim karissanti taraka* (*Jātaka* no. 49, *Nakkhatta-Jātaka*). Rather an interesting statement is made in *Jātaka* no. 431 to the effect that on some (unexplained) occasions, *ekaccesu thanesu, Bodhisattva* may destroy life, commit adultery, and drink intoxicants (*surā*); but they may not tell deceitful lies, *musāvādo,* which destroy the reality of things. Truth is the highest virtue. In mediaeval Sanskrit literature abstention from meat is a sign of virtue, as in the *Hitopadeśa,* where, more specifically, eating meat "on the Lord's day" is unlawful.

Here we face a question. Why do Buddhist advocate vegetarianism? The main reason is "mercy", and because we "cannot bear to eat the flesh of living creatures." And our belief in *kamma* tells us that we must eventually suffer the consequences of our evil actions. A Buddhist *Sutta* says : "The *Bodhisattva* fears the original action; the myriad of living creatures fear the consequences." This means that the Bodhisattva knows the seriousness of the consequences and does not do evil things; neither does he think about the causes of bad consequences. Finally, I also believe that a vegetarian diet better enables one to keep a pure body and mind and this purity is an important foundation of self-cultivation.

"Mercy" is an important way of learning to be a better person. Being without mercy is simply incompatible with being a Buddhist. Having a merciful and compassionate heart will show up in all aspects of one's life; but the simplest and most direct way is to follow a vegetarian diet. Think of the intense pain of accidentally stepping on a nail. So, how can one have the heart to eat the flesh of creatures who have suffered the pain of being slaughtered, skinned, dismembered and cooked? Being unable to bring ourselves to eat the flesh of these poor creatures is an expression of mercy.

I felt deeply moved reading two stories on the theme of mercy; they will remain etched forever in my memory. One is recorded in the book, *Record of Protecting Life* :

When a scholar named Chou Yu was cooking some eel to eat, he noticed one of the eels lifting its body so that its head and tail were still in the boiling liquid, but its arched upwards above the soup. It did not fall completely in until finally dying. Chou Yu found the occurrence a strange one and pulled out the eel, and cut it open. He found thousands of eggs inside. The eel had arched its belly out of the hot soup to protect its offspring. He cried at the sight, sighed with emotion and swore never to eat eel. This story tells us that the myriad living creatures are not without feeling and intelligence.

There is another story recorded in the Buddhist *Sutta* which goes like this—There was a king of heaven who was stalemated in a war with a demon and neither side emerged as winner. As the king was leading his soldiers back, he saw the nest of golden-winged bird in a tree by the roadside. "If the soldiers and chariots pass by here, the eggs in the nest will certainly fall to the ground and be scattered," he thought to himself. So he led his thousand chariots back the same road by which they came. When the demons saw the king returning, they fled in terror. The conclusion of the *Sutta* is that "if you use mercy to seek salvation, the Lord of heaven will see it." This story tells us that mercy may not seem like much at first glance, but it is in fact extremely powerful. The Buddhist *Suttas* frequently mention "the power of mercy." From this we know that mercy is indeed a potent force. If a Buddhist wants to learn to use this strength of mercy, he must be like the king of heaven in this story, and be ready to change the route of a thousand chariots rather than let a nest full of bird eggs fall to the ground.

The *Surangama Sutta* tells us that "if we eat the flesh of living creatures, we are destroying the seeds of compassion." That is, if we do not eat the flesh of living creatures, we are cultivating and irrigating the seeds of compassion," to "cultivate a compassionate heart."

In Buddhist teachings, volume upon volume have been written regarding cause and consequence, but the basic concept is a simple one. "Good is rewarded with good; evil is rewarded with evil; and the rewarding of good and evil is only a matter of time." Viewed from this concept, we will have to pay for every piece of flesh we eat with a piece of flesh, and with a life for every creature's life that we take. Viewed over a long term, eating meat is an extremely frightening prospect. Before their death, living creatures experience not joy, and not fear, but anger, not complaint, but hatred and resentment. The view point that all life is interrelated was used to promote abstention from meat eating within Buddhist control serves as the basis for protecting all animals.

Meat Eating in Mahayana Buddhism

The main reason why animals are killed is to provide food to those people who like to have meat as food. Buddhist texts and actions of Buddhist bhikkhus have sought to discourage this tendency. *Mahā-rājā-Kaniška-Lekha,* addressed to a hunting emperor, say : "Why do you commit such dreadful acts upon deer ? Your eyes are similar to the eyes of a young deer. When the deer are startled, they look about with eyeballs. Should you not therefore have compassion for these (deer)?[56]

The *Bodhisattva-bhumi,* a Mahāyāna Text states that the Bodhisattva's great generosity should not include giving away nets for catching animals or a piece of land on which animals might be hunted or killed. In the Mahāyāna tradition, Śāntideva had an aspiration that all should avoid meat,[57] and cited the Bodhisattva *Pātimokkha,* as saying that meat (flesh)—food should not be given to a bhikkhu, but if it was, he should eat it.[58] Some of the Mahāyāna texts give arguments for vegetarianism, such advocacy clearly having been facilitated by the climate of opinion that the Buddhist emphasis had helped to create. Thus, the Mahāyāna *Parinibbāna Sutta* says that eating meat 'extinguishes the seeds of great compassion[59] and has the Buddha explicitly saying', I order the various disciples from today that they cannot any more partake of meat'. This concept is also found in the *Lankāvatāra Sutta* in which a late section has a series of arguments against meat eating,[60] and has the Buddha denying the scriptural idea of it being 'blameless' to eat meat that is 'pure in three respects'. Such a direct contradiction of an earlier scriptural idea is unusual in Mahāyāna texts. The arguments of the *Sutta* can be summarized as follows :

(i) All beings in some past lives have been one's close relatives such as one's mother or friend. One should look on all beings as if they were one's own children and not eat them.

(ii) The smell of a meat eater frightens other beings and also gives a bad reputation.

(iii) Meat eating by Buddhists means the *Dhamma* will be spoken ill of and the *Bodhisattva* will lose their listeners.

(iv) Meat stinks

(v) Meat eating prevents meditation and leads to arrogance, as do onions, garlic, alcohol etc.

(vi) Meat eaters sleeps uneasily.

(vii) Meat eating leads to a bad rebirth as a carnivorous animal or a low caste human.

The *Sutta* concludes that it is Kammically fruitful to avoid flesh food and that the arguments defending meat eating are spurious and that the Buddha never ate meat.

The *Mahāyāna Suttas* including the *Lankāvatāra Sutta,* the *mahāparinibbāna Sutta,* and the *Brahmajāla Sutta,* unmistakably condemn meat eating.

According to the *Lankavātāra Sutra* : "For the sake of love of purity, the *Bodhisattva* should refrain from eating flesh, which is born of semen, blood, etc. For fear of causing terror to living beings let the *Bodhisattva,* who is disciplining himself to attain compassion, refrain from eating flesh... It is not true that meat is proper food and permissible when the animal was not killed by himself, when he did not order others to kill it, when it was not specially meant for him... Again, there may be some people in the future who... being under the influence of the taste for meat will string together in various ways sophistic arguments to defend meat eating. Meat eating in any form, in any manner, and at any place is unconditionally and once for all prohibited. Meat eating I have not permitted to anyone, I do not permit, I will not permit".[61]

Similarly in the *Surangama Sutta,* it is pointed out thus : "The reason for practising *Dhyāna* and seeking to attain *Samādhi* is to escape from the sufferings of life, but in seeking to escape from suffering ourselves why should we inflict it upon others? Unless you can so control your minds that even the thought of brutal unkindness and killing is abhorrent, you will never be able to escape from the bondage of the world's life... After my *Parinibbāna* in the last *kappa* different kinds of ghosts will be encountered everywhere deceiving people and teaching them that they can eat meat and still attain enlightenment... How can a bhikkhu, who hopes to become a deliverer of others, himself be living on the flesh of other sentient beings?"[62]

The *Mahāparinibbāna Sutta* also condemns meat eating. "The eating of meat extinguishes the seed of great passion." How is that the Mahāyāna teachings directly contradict those of the *Theravāda* in the matter of meat-eating? It become all the more puzzling when one realizes that the Sanskrit scriptures were contemporary or nearly so, with the Pāli scriptures.

Vegetarianism is the only way through which one can stop the habit of eating meat. People may choose vegetarian diet because of a variety of philosophical, religious and ethical beliefs. Some people abstain from meat eating for religious reasons. For example, Jainas, and some Buddhists and some Hindus believe that he killing of animals violates the ethical precept of *ahiṃsā* or non-violence. Ecological reasons motivate other people, because much less land is required to raise vegetables and grains than live stocks.

The *Lankāvatāra Sutta* also includes stories to emphasize the need for vegetarianism. The text states that "even Indra who had obtained sovereignty over the gods had once to assume the form of hawk owing to his habit of eating meat for food in a previous existence. It then tells of a king who was taken by his wife into a forest. After wandering about in it, he committed evil deeds with a lioness out of fear for his life, and children were born to her. Because of their descending from the union with a lioness, the royal children were called 'spotted-feet' etc. On account of their habit in the past when their food had been flesh, they ate meat even after becoming kings and ... because they were excessively attached and devoted to meat-eating, they gave births to *Ḍākās* and *Ḍākinīs* who were terrible eaters of human flesh. In the life after transmigration... such ones will fall into the wombs of such excessive flesh-devouring creatures as the lion, the tiger, the panther, the wolf, the hyaena, the wild-cat, the jackal, the owl, etc. They will fall into the wombs of still more greedily flesh-devouring and still more terrible *Rākkshasa* (demons).

The eighth chapter of the *Lankāvatāra Sutta* answers many objections to the requirement that all Buddhists bhikkhus be vegetarians. It states that those who teach that the Buddha allowed meat eating or that he himself died from eating bad meat are wrong. The discourse includes the following assertion :

The food for my *Srāvakas, Pratyekabuddhas,*
And *Bodhisattvas* is the *Dhamma* and not
How much more the *Tathāgata!*
The *Tathāgata* is the *Dhammakāya,*
Mahāmati; he abides in the *Dhamma*
on food; his is not a
Body feeding on flesh, he does not
Abide by in any flesh food. He has
Ejected the habit-energy of thirst
And desire which sustain all
Existence; he is all-seer;

He regards all beings impartially as his own children; he is a great compassionate heart. Mahāmati, having regarded all beings as my own children how can I permit the *srāvakas* to eat the flesh of their own children, much less my eating it? That I have permitted the *Srāvakas* as well to partake of (meat-eating), Mahāmati, has no foundation whatever.

This eighth chapter of the *Lankāvatāra Sutra* ends with twenty four verses which advocate vegetarianism. Some of the important verses are given below.

Verse 2 : Meat is not agreeable to the wise; it has a nauseating odour, it causes a bad reputation, it is food for the carnivores; I say this Mahāmati; it is not to be eaten.

Verse 14 : (The meat-eater) is ill smelling, contemptuous and born deprived of intelligence; he will be born again and again among the families of the *candata,* the *pukkana* and the *Domb.*

Verse 23 : (Meat-eating) is forbidden by me everywhere and all the time for those who are abiding in compassion; (he who eats meat) will be born in the some place as the lion, the tiger, the wolf, etc.

Verse 24 : Therefore do not meat which will cause terror among people, because it hinders the truth of emancipation; (not to eat meat), this is the mark of the wise.

The *Dasabhumikā Sutta* another important Mahāyāna text, states that a Buddhist "must not hate any being and cannot kill a living creature even in thought. Kśemendra writes" I cannot endure the pain even of an ant.

Now here, I would like to discuss about the early Buddhist attitude towards animal sacrifice in Buddhism. First of all, I will try to understand the meaning of sacrifice. 'Sacrifice' is usually defined as the slaughter of an animal or a person or the surrender of possession as an offering to a deity; the original meaning, 'to make sacred' may be applied to all kinds of rituals. In sacrifice, the offering is identified with the deity. Thus, in the slaying of the animal, the deity is slain. The ritualistic principle that the worshipper becomes identified with the deity in order to exercise the same control over the nature as the deity is involved in sacrifice in that the worshipper is the victim at his own sacrifice. In the sacrificial process the victim may baseline in various ways like it may be strangled or clubbed or have its throat cut, etc.

An obvious abuse of animals, during the time of the Buddha, was the killing of them as part of elaborate brahmanical sacrificial rituals. The Buddha, along with the leaders of other non-brahmanical renunciative groups was very critical of this because of the cruelty involved and also because it did not bring about the objectives the brahmans hoped for. Rejecting the brahmanic view of it as a wholesome act leading to a happy rebirth, he saw it as having the opposite qualities.[63] Such criticism led to a great decrease in the use of animals in this way. The Buddha praised brahmans of old for not sacrificing animals—probably historically correct and in the *Kutādanta Sutta*,[62] describes sacrifice which he had himself conducted for a king in past life. In this, no animals were killed, no trees were felled to act as sacrificial posts, no workmen were forced to help, and the only offerings were items such as butter and honey.[65] Such a description was clearly meant as a contrast to the then mode of sacrificing animals.

The *Kutādanta Sutta* of *Digha Nikāya* mainly discusses the wrong and the right way of sacrifice. In this sutta the mode of right and wrong sacrifice is clearly described. In order to ensure that not even one minor mistake is made regarding technical details for the accurate performance of the sacrifice to which the god was supposed to attach great weight, the intending sacrificer is ironically represented as doing the very last thing any brahman under similar circumstances would think of doing. The *Kutādanta Brahman* goes to the Buddha for advice about the modes of the ritual to be performed at the sacrifice and about the requisite utensils, the altar furniture etc. to be used in performing it.

The Buddha's answer is to tell him a wonderful legend of a king Mahāvīgīta (wide-realm) and of a truly the most extraordinary sacrifice imaginable he offered. All its marvellous details, each one settled, be it noted, on the advice of a brahman, are described with a deliberate extravagance, nonetheless delicious because of the evident earnestness of the moral to be inferred. The three modes in which the ritual is to be performed are declared to be simply three conditions of mind, or rather one condition of mind at three different times, i.e. harbouring of no regrets either before or during or after the sacrifice at the expenditure involved. It is the hearty co-operation with the king of four divisions of his people, the nobles, the officials, the brahmans and the householders that makes four articles of furniture. The king himself had to have eight personal qualification which are as follows :

(i) He was well born from both sides i.e. on the mother's and the father's side.

(ii) He was handsome, of pleasant appearance, inspiring trust, fine in presence etc.

(iii) He was mighty, with great wealth and property with stores of silver and gold etc.

(iv) He was powerful and in command of an army which was loyal and disciplined, and also an able commander.

(v) He was a kind hearted, generous, noble giver and a doer of good deeds.

(vi) He knew the meaning of what had been said, and could explain it clearly.

(vii) He was learned in all kinds of knowledge.

(viii) He was intelligent, expert and wise and able to think out things present or past or future.[66]

Apart from these eight personal qualification of the king himself, the four personal qualifications of his advising brahman make up the total of the sixteen articles required. No living thing either animal or vegetable is to be injured. The sacrifice is offered on behalf, not only of the king himself, but of all the good people. And the uttering of mystic verses over each article used and over mangled and bleeding bodies of unhappy victims, verses on which all the magic efficacy of the sacrifices had been supposed to depend, is quietly ignored.

Except in the last paragraph of the *Kutādanta Sutta,* there is nothing exclusively Buddhistic. That a sacrifice of heart is better than a sacrifice of bullocks (animals), the ethical more worthy than any physical sacrifice, is simply the sensible and rational human view. The Vedic sacrifices of animals had practically been given up when the long struggle between Brahmanism and Buddhism reached its close. Isolated instances of such sacrifices are known even down to the Islamic invasion. But the battle was really won by the Buddhists and the combined ridicule and the earnestness of our *Sutta* must have had its share in bringing about the victory.

We find many instances in the *Jātaka* stories where the sacrifice of living creatures or things is forbidden. One of such stories is named *Ayakutā Jātaka.*[67] According to the story, there was a king named Brahmadutta who was the ruler of Benāras and Bodhisattva came to life as the son of his chief queen. After his father, he became the king of Banāras. At that time people were devoted to worship of the gods and made religious offerings to them by slaughtering goats, rams and other like animals. The Bodhisattva proclaimed to the beat of drum : "No living creature is to be put to death". The *Yakkhas* were enraged against the Bodhisattva at losing their offerings. They called up an assembly and decided to kill the Bodhisattva and to fulfil this mission they sent forth a certain *yakkha.* He took a huge blazing mass of iron and went and stood near the bed-head of the Bodhisattva. At that time the throne of Sakka manifested signs of heat and after considering the matter the god discovered the cause and grasping his thunderbolt in his hand, he came and stood over the *Yakkha.* When the Bodhisattva saw the *Yakkha* he wondered why he was standing there. Was it to protect or to slay him? He had seen only the *Yakkha* and not Sakka. The *Yakkha* because of fear of Sakka was not bale to slay him and he said to the Bodhisattva that he was stationed there not to guard but to slay him. But the *Yakkha* was not able to slay him returned to his place of abode. That the sacrifice of living creatures is forbidden is also discussed in *Jātaka* No.-433, named *Lomasakassapa Jātaka.* There are many more *Jātaka* stories where I come across with the description of sacrifices and the offerings of sacrifices etc. I have also been able to find some *Suttas* in Buddhist literature which are mainly concerned with sacrifices.

These are as follows :

Māgha, make offering (he said),
But in so doing, cleanse thy heart
In all its ways, to the offerer
The offering in the help; by this
Supported, he doth them quilt bate
With passion gone and hate expelled
Let him in boundless measure them
Quicken a heart of mity (love)
E'er day and night with zeal suffere
All quarters to infinite.
Who offers, Māgha (he then said),
The offering three fold[68] endowed,
He would make offerings prosperous
By giving to gift-worthy-men,

And rightly minded, offering thus.
They ready almoner doth rise
Unto the world of Brahman, I say

Sutta Nipāta, 506, 507, & 509.

Wherefore, brahman, bend low thine ear, and *Dhamma* will, teach :

Ask not of birth but of the faring ask!
From wood is awe inspiring fire begot;
From lowly clan noble becomes the sage
Who's steadfast and by modesty restrained.

Truth tamed endued with temperance, adept
In lore and end, has the Brahma-faring fared;
Timely on him let brahman seeking merit
In sacrifice his offering bestow.

On them who, lust forsaking, homeless free,
The well controlled of self, on shuttle straight
Timely on them let brahman seeking merit
In sacrifice his offering bestow.

The passion less with faculties composed
And freed no moon from Rahu's dark eclipse
Timely on them let brahman seeking merit
In sacrifice his offering bestow.

Those unattached who way fare in the world
The ever mindful, quit of thoughts of 'mine'
Timely on them let brahmana seeking merit
In sacrifice his offering bestow.

He who is pleasure quit, as conqueror fares
Hath found and known the end of birth and death
Cool man, cool as the waters of a lake,
Oblation-worthy is the man thus come.

Peer with his peers, aloof from crooked men
Of boundless wisdom is the man thus come
Unsoiled by anything of there or hence,
Oblation-worthy is the man thus come.

In whom abide the neither guile nor pride,
He who is free of greed 'and mine' and hope
Void of all wrath, exceeding cool of self.
A brahman he, with stain of sorrow razed
oblation worthy is the man thus come.

He who hath, razed all harbours of the mind
In whom abides no claim to things whatever
He, unattached to things of here or hence
Oblation worthy is the man thus come.

He who with mind intent hath crossed the flood
And *Dhamma* in the fondmost view hath known.

The cankkerless who his last body bears,
Oblation worthy is the man thus come.

In who becoming, conkers, all harsh speech,
Are quenched, gone to their end, and are no more.

He lose adept, released in every way,
Oblation-worthy is the man thus come.

Mid men of pride, no man of pride himself,
Bond overcome who bath no bounds left,
Who understand deth ill, its base and scope,
Oblation worthy is the man thus come

Seer of the lone, not trusting here to hope
Who view and love of the other men hath passed
He is whom no supports whatever exist,
Oblation-worthy is the man thus come.

He who hath reached the you and high of things,
So all are ended, quenched and are no more,
Clam man, and in attachment's end released
Oblation worthy is the man thus come.

Seer of the end and turn of bond and birth,
Who passion's ways later wholly left behind.
The cleansed, spotless, taintless, without flow,
Oblation worthy is the man thus come.

He who perceiveth not self by the self,
Intent-of-mind, straight-goer poised-of-self
He truly still, the vital, doubt free man,
Oblation worthy is the man thus come.

He with no room for error whatsoever,
The seer of knowledge on to all that is.

He who his final body beneath now
Won to the full awakening, utter bliss.
(Such is he cleansing of that spirit here)
Oblation worthy is he man thus come.

Not mine t'enjoy fare won from chanting hymns,
Tis not the things of seers, o brahmana?
Far wom from chanting hymns the wake reject,
Where *Dhamma* reigns this, brahman is the rule

May, thou must offer other food and drink
To a great *risi* wholly consumanate
The cankkerless, untroubled man of calm
Sure field is that for merit-seeking man

Him th' unprovokable.
Him of unclonded mind,
Freed of all lustfulness,
Void of all indolence,
Guide of those on he brink,
Master of birth and death,
Type of the silent sage
Perfect in silent lore
Come to the sacrifice :
Him with thy brows unknit
Venerate with joined hands
Worship with food and drink.
Thus prosper holy sifts

Sutta Nipāta-462-478, 480-481 & 483-485

Whoever month by month should sacrifice
For a century with a thousand (offerings)
But should venerate even for a moment
One who has made the self become
That veneration is better than oblation
for a hundred years
And whoever may tend for a century
The (sacred) fire in the (sacrificial) grove,
But should venerate even for a moment
One who has made the self become
That veneration is better than oblation
for a hundred years

Dhammapada. 106-107

Nay, brahman, deem not that by mere wood-laying
Comes purity, verily that is external
To him who thus purification seeketh
By things without none is made pure, the wise say.

I lay no wood, brahman, for fires on altars,
Only within burneth the flame I kindle.
Ever my fire burns, ever compared-of-self,
I perfected, fare the Brahma-faring.
As load of fuel surely is pride, brahman.
The altar's smoke, anger, thy false words, ashes,
The tongue's the priest's spoon; and the heart
of the altar;
The flame thereon - this is man's self well tamed,
A lake is *Dhamma*, with virtue's strend for bathing,
Clear, undefiled, praised by the good to good men,
Wherein in sooth masters of lose come bathing,

So, clean of limb, to the beyond cross over.
Dhamma is truth, restraint is Brahma-faring,
The middle way pursuing, brahman, the way to
Brahma attainment.
Due honour pay thou to the upright-minded.
Whose doth this, him do I call Tide-rider.[69]

I have found some references in the Anguttara Nikaya on sacrifical fire which is as follows :[69a]

"Brahman, even before the (animal) sacrifice a man who lays the fire, who sets up the pillar, sets up three swords, evil, ill in yield, ill in fruit. What three ? The deed-sword, the word-sword, the thought-sword".

Even before the sacrifice, brahman, a man laying the fire, setting up the pillar, causes such thoughts to arise as : "Let there be slain for the sacrifice so many bulls, so many steers, heifers, goats, rams!" Thinking to make merit, he makes demerit; thinking to do good, he does evil; thinking he seeks the way of happy going, he seeks the way of ill-going. Brahman, even before the sacrifice, a man laying the fire, setting up the pillar sets up firstly this thought-sword, which is evil, ill in yield, ill in fruit.

Again, brahman, even before the sacrifice, a man... speaks thus : "Let there be slain so many bulls, steers, heifers, goats and rams!" Thinking to make merit, he makes demerit;... he seeks the way of ill-going. Brahman, even before the sacrifice, he, laying the fire, setting up the pillar, sets up secondly this word-sword.

Moreover, Brahman, even before the sacrifice, a man laying the fire, setting up the pillar, himself first sets on foot the business, saying : "Let them slay bulls, steers, heifers, goats, rams!" Thinking to make merit, he makes demerit... he seeks the way of ill-going. Brahman, even before the sacrifice, he laying the fire, setting up the pillar, sets up thirdly this deed-sword. These three evil swords are ill in yield, ill in fruit.

Brahman, these three fires ought to be forsaken, shunned

and avoided. What three? The fires of passion, hatred and delusion. And why ought these fires to be forsaken, shunned and avoided? With mind impassioned (perverted or deluded), mastered, obsessed by passion (hatred or delusion) he takes a course ill in act, word and thought; and so doing, on the breaking up of the body after dying, he arises in the waste, the Bad Bourn, the Downfall, *Niraya Hell.* Therefore, these three fires ought to be forsaken, shunned and avoided.

Brahman, these three following fires when esteemed, revered, venerated, respected, must bring perfect happiness. What three? The fires of the venerable, the householder, the gift-worthy.

And what is the fire of the venerable? Consider, brahman, the man who honours his mother and father—this is called the fire of the venerable. And why? From this, this veneration has sprung. Therefore, brahman, the fire of the venerable when esteemed, revered, venerated, respected, must bring perfect happiness.

And what is the fire of the householder? Consider, the brahman, the man who honours his sons, womenfolk, slaves, messengers, workmen—this is called the fire of the householder. Therefore, the fire of the householder when esteemed... must bring perfect happiness.

And what is the fire of the gift-worthy? Consider, brahman, those recluses and brahmans who abstain from pride indolence, who bear things, patiently and meekly, each taming self, each calming self, each making self attain utter *nibbāna*[70]—this is called the fire of gift-worthy. Therefore, brahman, this fire of the gift-worthy when esteemed, revered, venerated, respected, must bring perfect happiness.

No brahman, I do not praise every sacrifice. Yet I do not withhold praise from every sacrifice. In whatever sacrifice are slaughtered cows, goats and sheep, fowl and swine, and where diverse living creatures come to destruction, such sacrifice, brahman, as involves butchery, I do not praise. Why? To such a sacrifice involving butchery, neither perfected ones nor those who have entered the way to perfection draw near. But in whatever sacrifice cows are not slaughtered, nor goats and sheep, nor fowl and swine, and where divers living creatures do not come to destruction, such sacrifice not involving butchery, I do praise, such ass, for example, a long established charity for the welfare of the clan. Why? Because to such a sacrifice, which involves no butchery both perfected ones and those who have entered the way to perfection draw near. Buddhism never praised sacrifices of animals or any living creature, which is quite clear from one of the *Sutta* of *Anguttara Nikāya,*[70a] which is as follows :

> The sacrifice called the "Horse", the "man",
>
> The "Throwing of the peg", the "Drinking Rite",
>
> The "House unbarred[71] with all their cruelty
>
> Have little fruit. Where goats and sheep and line of drivers sorts are scarified go not
>
> Those sages great who've travelled the right way.
>
> But sacrifices free from cruelty.
>
> Which men deep up for profit of the clan,
>
> Where goats and sheep and kine of divers sorts
>
> Are never sacrificed, to such as these
>
> Go sages great who've travelled the right way.
>
> Such should the thoughtful celebrate; and great
>
> The fruits of such profit, they bring not loss.
>
> Lavish the offering, *devas* therewith are pleased.
>
> A.II. 42-43

From the above discussion, one can clearly say that the Buddha was totally against sacrifices performed by brahmanas. Once a king had sixteen dreadful dreams and consulted brahmanas, who suggested to sacrifice animals and birds to avoid the evil, prophesied by the dreams. On the insistence of the queen, the king went to the Buddha and related to him the dreams and the means suggested by the brahmanas, to avoid the evil. The Buddha replied, "To undo the effect of the dreams, sacrifice is not the remedy. It will on the contrary only double the evil effect." This story is told in the *Mahāsupinā Jātaka*. Sacrifice was started by the corrupt brahmanas and they became demoralised and coveted the riches and the kine. They suggested to the kings to offer sacrifices, who being won over by them offered sacrifices of horses etc.[72] On account of sacrificing innocent kine, which formerly were respected for being abundantly useful and health giving, diseases which of yore were only three, rose to ninety-eight.[73] Once the Buddha was in Śrāvasti and at that time a great sacrifice was arranged to be held for the king, Prasenjit. Five hundred bulls, five hundred bullocks and many heifers, goats and rams were led to the pillar to be sacrificed. Slaves, menials and craftsmen hectored about by blows and by fear, made the preparation with tearful faces. A number of almsmen saw the preparation for the sacrifice and related the matter to the Buddha. The Buddha said, "Sacrifice the horse, the man and the beast does not bring a rich result. The sages do not attend a rite where diverse goats, sheep and kine are slain. But sage attend such sacrifices where no goats, sheep and kine are slain. Such rites entail great results".[74]

Buddhism is a universal religion. Compassion, non-violence and loving kindness are the root concepts of Buddhist philosophy and religion. Its universality and appeal depends upon its emphasis on compassion and loving kindness as everything is possessed of the Buddha nature. Killing in all forms have been forbidden because of Buddhist Astrology. *Ahimsa* and *Karuna* became so pronounced in early Buddhism that these two concepts were instrumental in taking Buddhism to the masses and making it a universal religion.

REFERENCES

1. Vin. I. 237-38.
2. Commentary on Vin. III. 604-06.
3. M.I. 386-87
4. SBE. III. 155.
5. SBE. XI. 196ff; BD.I. 297ff.
6. C.S. Singh, 'Meat Eating and the Rule of Tikotiparisudha' A.K. Narain (ed.) *Studies in Pali and Buddhism*, Delhi (1979) 289-295.
7. M. I. 80.

8. A. I. 221.
9. MLS. II. 33; BD. I. 298.
10. J. II. 182.
11. D. II. 5.
12. SBE. XVII. 49.
13. BD. I. 98.
14. SBE. VII. 43.
15. Pātimokkha, Pacittiya Dhamma No. 33.
16. SBE. XVII. 85.
17. C.S. Prasad, *Logic Behind Allowing Meat Eating and Prohibiting it in Buddhism* (1971), p. 104-05.
18. DB. II. 137.
19. Vin. II. 171-2.
20. *Dialogues of the Buddha,* II. 137.
21. *PED : S.V. Sukara.*
22. Ibid.
23. JRAS : 1906; 656, 881.
24. *sampanna-kolan sukaramaṃsa* (poork with jujube) at A. III. 49.
25. D.B. II. 137.
26. Ivan Morris, *Madly Singing in the Mountains : An Appreciation and Anthology of Arthur Waley.* 342.
27. Quoted at R.p. Kapleau : 24.
28. J. VI. 531.
29. Edward Thomas, *The Life of the Buddha,* London : Routledge, (1949), p. 149.
30. C.A.F. Rhys Davids, *A Manual of Buddhism,* London : Sheldon, (1932) 260.
31. SBE. II. XXVII. 88.
32. Henry S. Salt, "The Humanities of Diet," in Tom Regan & Peter Singer (Eds), *Animal Rights and Human Obligations.* Eaglewood Cliffs. NJ : Prentice Hall, (1976), p. 143-44.
33. Milinda Pañhā. IV. 3.22
34. SBE. XXXV. 244.
35. J. III. 289.
36. Ibid. 462.
37. J. VI. 23, 9ff.
38. J. III. 322.
39. In JRAS. Jan. 1906.
40. J. V. 20.
41. J. V. 235.
42. J. IV. 273.
43. J. IV. 437.
44. J. I. 159, 491.
45. J. IV. 371.

46. J. III. 527, J. 1, 22.
47. J. II. 245.
48. J. I. 41.
49. J. II. 153.
50. J. II. 377.
51. Hardy's Manual, p. 327.
52. JRAS. July, 1906, p. 584, J. V. 237.
53. J. V. 458.
54. J. I. 275.
55. J. I. 205, lines 1 and 7 to Sujata.
56. *Ārya-Satyaka-Parivarata*-translated by L. Jamspal. *The Range of the Bodhisattva : A Study of an Early Mahāyāna Sutra. Discourse of the truth teller*, p. 71-72.
57. Śāntideva, Śikṣā-Samucchaya, p. 33.
58. Ibid., p. 143.
59. R.P. Kapleau, *To Cherish All Life : A Buddhist view of Animals Slaughter and Meat Eating*, Rouchester, NY, The Zen Centre (1981), p. 34.
60. D.T. Suzuki, The *Lankāvatāra Sutra*, 1982, p. 211-223.
61. *The Lankāvatāra Sūtra*, tr. D. Suzuki, London : Routledge : 1932.
62. *A Buddhisst Bible*, ed. Dwight Goddard, New York : Dutton : 1952 : 264-65.
63. A. II. 42.
64. D. I. 127-49.
65. D. I. 141.
66. Buddhaghosha explains this as meaning that he knew the result of *kamma*, he knew that his present prosperity was a gift to him by the good deeds done to others in the past and that there would be a similar result in the future for his good deeds done now.
67. J. III. 347, 96-97.
68. A. III. 36. Here the meaning of three fold offering is explained as where the giver's part is three fold—(i) before the gift he is glad at heat, (ii) in giving the heart is satisfied and (iii) uplifted is the hart wehen he has given.
69. Similar version given by Mrs. Rhys Davids in KS. I. 212, S.I. 168.

69a. A. IV. 42-45.

70. Parinibbapenti—'Taming, calming, making one self attain nirvāṇa', also mentioned at A. I. 168, A. II. 68, A. II. 46 and D. III. 61.

72a. A. II. 42-43.

71. These sacrifices are also referred to at A.IV, 151.
72. Sn. 73-75.
73. Ibid.
74. KS. I. 102, (SBB)

Chapter-4

ANIMAL RIGHTS AND BUDDHISM

During the late 20th century many tacitly accepted relationships between humans and the environment have come under scrutiny. One need only look as far as the local newspaper or sporting goods shows, to find evidence of tension between communities that extract natural resources and those that attempt to proscribe them. From concerns about logging to protests over endagered species, environmental concerns and moral behaviour of human beings towards them permeate modern society. Nowhere do these concerns appear more contentious than in the realm of human and non-human animal relationships. Due to all these happenings, one can easily notice that there is evidence of an emerging mass movement that questions the morality of human beings who interact with animals.

Actually, the animal rights movement attempts to protect animals from human exploitation. The movement is an intellectual and cultural phenomenon that has landed on modern western culture's front porch. Like a newborn child abandoned on the doorstep, its seemingly sudden, unanticipated appearance and loud cries have left casual observers startled and perplexed, wondering "where did it come from?" "Why is it here?", "To whom does it belong?" and "what can be done now"? It did not spring full blown from the brow of contemporary philosophers and intellectuals. Rather, the movement has a historical precendent and, like its predecessor, the contemporary animal rights advocates carry the symbolic cause of animals out of the laboratory beyond the barnyard gate and into the realm of human activity. The animal rights movement is marked by utilitarianism and moral rights philosophy is located within the middle class, and is currently notable for the diversity of its criticism. The underlying causes for the movement's emergence and rapid growth include a unique convergence of four factors which are :

(a) Rapid urbanization

(b) Scientific evidence linking animals and people

(c) Changes in the anthropomorphic images of animals and

(d) Ascendancy of equalitarianism as a universal political value.

The animal rights movement poses many questions regarding relationships between animals and human beings. Indeed, animal rights activists ask, "If science tells us that we are related to other animals and they are very similar to us, and if my experience tells me that animals are similar to us, then why should not we extend protection to animals?" This questions has already had a profound impact on human behaviour involving animals and the answer will continue to affect human behaviour in future.

The transformation of animals into objects of commodity production and profit extraction, and the alienation and objection of animals has reached its apex.[1] Animals have become mere objects and instruments for human use in this modern age. The treatment of animals as objects is intimately connected with the view, deeply entrenched in western culture and its discourse, of sharp discontinuity between humans and animals. This picture dictates that humans, as subjects live in a world of culture and freedom, while animals as subjects inhabit a realm of necessity, positivity and compulsion. But scholars are of different views regarding the rights of animals. One group of scholars is of the view that creatures have no rights. This school is represented by Hugo Grotics, Someul von Pufendorf and Christian Thomasius. They reinforce traditional Christian as well as Cartesian anthropocentrism which is the main doctrine of this school of thought. According to this school of thought, law has developed within a community of rational beings for the purpose of regulating their social relations. Being regarded as irrational creatures, animals do not fall within the system of natural rights. This point of view was expounded by Pufendorf. He is of the view that humans have no legal or contractual obligations towards animals. This is not a new doctrine in itself because when we go into antiquity one can find that the Stoic Philosophers had already taken a similar view. They in their view had already denied that animals were endowed with reason and had therefore advocated the unlimited right of man to make use of animals.[2] In the 17th century, philosophers like Hobbes and Spinoza had also provided arguments that the animals were "creatures without rights'. According to Hobbes, the absence of rationality and speech in animals meant that they were unable to make a particular being depended on its 'virtue and power' which means that human beings had far more rights over animals than animals over man. This idea that animals had no rights at all provoked opposition.

The Nuremberg philosopher Apinus spoke of a great controversy among scholars concerning the question of "whether one has duties towards animals." Apinus introduced some valuable ideas concerning human rights over animals. He agreed with the view the humans have no legal or contractual obligation towards animals but he stressed that animals were objects of human duties to God. These duties include "conservation of animals" and respect for God's direction of animals to their purposes'. The first principle meant that it was man's duty to care for domestic animals and to abstain from killing or hurting animals without necessity. And according to the second principle, it was forbidden to mutilate an animal, for this would mean disregard for its God-given design. So Apinus constructed indirect obligations towards animals which resulted from direct obligations to God. Another philosopher of this century named David Hume put forward another concept of indirect obligations in his enquiry concurring the principles of morals in which he denied that man and animals could form a 'society' because this would presuposse a degree of equality'. Hume was of the view that animals were inferior to human beings, both physically and mentally, even though he stressed that man should be bound by the laws of humanity to give gentle usage to these creatures.[3] Thus, he advanced an obligation within the human community. At the same time, Immanuel Kant thought that the treatment of animals was nothing but man's duty to himself. There was an indirect obligation to abstain from violence and cruelty towards animals because of the fact that man's compassion for suffering human beings might be weakened and gradually obliterated.[4] The conception of indirect obligation more or less restricted human rights over animals compared to Pufendorf's view of man's relationship to the animal world. Still, the basic doctrine of the school of natural rights that animals were creatures without rights was never challenged by these concepts or doctrines. Yet, in the second half of the 18th century, some philosophers or thinkers broke with this doctrine.

The Glasgow philosopher Francis Hatcheson in his book, '*System of Moral Philosophy*' (1755) declared that animals had the right that no useless pain should be inflicted upon them, even though he was of the view that they 'can have no right... against mankind in anything necessary for human support.' Another similar view was taken by a Swiss scholar and naturalist Charles Bonnet that a divine order existed in nature and that the purpose of this divine order consisted in the greatest possible happiness 'of sentient and of thinking beings,,' which means that it was immoral to treat a sentient being like an insensible one or 'an animal like a pebble stone. Bonnet did not actually speak of animal rights as such, yet he expressed the ideas that every sentient being had some sort of claim to happiness in its life.

Another scholar named Hamphrey Primatt took a decisive step towards animals' right to happiness. He was of the view that the suffering of animals was worse than that of human beings because animals had no hope of a future life. Moreover, as speechless creatures they were unable to accuse their tormentors and as irrational beings they could not endure pain on punishment. By this point of view, one thing is clearly said that the faculty to suffer pain had become a new criterion for the concession of rights. So, Primatt attacked the old criterion of rationality. According to Primatt, it was quite clear that man did not have a natural right to abuse or torture an animal just because it did not possess the mental powers of a human being.

Primatt's argument foreshadowed the much better known plea for the acknowledgement of animal rights by Jeremy Bentham. His famous dictum on the question is not, 'can they reason'? Nor 'can they talk'? But 'can they suffer'?[5] He compared the status of animals with that of the slaves and argued for the existence of animal rights just as for the abolition of slavery. Bentham was of the view that the faculty to suffer pain with the complementary faculty to feel pleasure was the central principle. He criticised ancient jurists who had degraded animals to mere things and had neglected their interests. A very similar point of view was propounded by Wilhem Dietler. He cricised the traditional view that animals were creatures without rights as a very wooden philosophy. Lack of rationality in animals and their inability to lodge their claims were not sufficient reasons to deny the existence of animal rights :

"Of course, if one concedes rights only to someone who is capable of taking legal steps against us, one has reason to deny them to animals, for they will hardly appear against us in court because of offences. But a minor child is unable to do this either and still one does not deny that it is illegal, unjust, to kill a child, to hurt it and so on, i.e. that the child has certain rights. Accordingly animals can have rights as well, which means that certain actions against them can be unjust and forbidden".[6]

The whole theory that animals had rights formulated by Primatt, Bentham and Dietler, was surely an alternative to the concept of indirect obligation towards animals as advocated by Apinus, Hume and Kant. Corresponding to the concept of indirect obligation towards animals, the danger of brutalization through cruelty to animals was a vital aspect. The argument that animals had no rights because they had no idea about rights and obligations was not valid. Before the nineteenth century a jurist of Leipzig named Karl F. Hommel came forth with the idea of animal rights. He dealt with the general legal problems of cruelty to animals. He did not share the opinion that human beings had no legal obligations to animals and he further argued that under this presupposition there would be no obligations to the foetus and to the small child either, since they were also unable to make demands. He defined duty in a broader sense as 'an action which the law of nature demands of us'. On this basis he propounded an idea of an indirect obligation to animals derived from a direct duty to God. He substantiated the latter with the theological view that God wished the well-being of all his creatures and that He had created the world for happiness and pleasure of all beings. Hommel's conclusion reflected in his rituals which read as follows :

"So I state natural obligations of human beings towards animals and so to written law. I do not hesitate to number cruelty against animals among those crises which are described as crimina extraordinaria, and which the judge average with an arbitrary punishment though the law is silent on this point".[8]

The changes described in the theological and the philosophical views of the man-animal relationship obviously reflect the development of somewhat more friendly climate for animals in the 18th century. A number of contemporary intellectuals were certainly prepared to assume a less anthropocentric attitude than had prevailed in the 16th and the 17th centuries. Yet it has to be observed that such kindness to the 'brute creation' was still confined to the educated elite. In fact even in the late 18th century, the position of intellectuals pleading for considerate treatment of animals still seems to have been rather a weak one. Seen against this background, contemporary comments on the ethics of the man-animal relationship may appear little more than 'straws in the wind'.[9] Yet it would not be appropriate to interpret them as mere expositions of individual over-sensitivity. In the 17th and the 18th centuries, the ground was evidently prepared for the rise of the humane movement of the nineteenth century.

Historians and social scientists trace the origin of contemporary animal rights movement to the nineteenth century's Anti-vivisection Movement. The movement arose out of profound social reaction to increasing technological change and was concerned with the symbolic position of animals as liaison between recently urbanized people and nature. Originally a puritan reaction to both the Industrial Revolution and Victorian Materialism, the Anti-Vivisection Movement responded to the perception of increasing human exploitation of and intrusion into the natural world. Social scientists have discovered that during periods of intense technology change and social displacement there has often been receptivity to criticism of forces in society that appear responsible for the change. Hence, whether in the realm of agriculture or industry, technology came to be identified as the culprit. When placed in this context, the Anti-Vivisection Movements of the 19th and the 20th centuries as the current animal rights movement reflect widespread and deeply felt anxiety regarding social change. The Victorian Anti-Vivisection Movement used sensationalized publicity along with exposes of animal mistreatment and apocalyptic literature to mobilize public sentiment against animal experimentation, animal baiting, and the use of animals in sports. The movement depended heavily on aristocratic noblesse oblige as a reservoir of support, and played heavily upon public sensibilities concerning morality and brutality. The Victorian movement had little impact upon the use of animals. Eventually, the movement disintegrated. However, the symbolic reaction against the utilization of animals did not disappear altogether. The movements radical agenda for the transformation of society eventually dissolved into the social milieu, leaving the reformist animal welfare movement as its legacy. Welfare groups carried the torch-seeking to abate animal suffering and anti-vivisection sentiments emerged briefly in the 1950's in the form of social reaction to various scientific phenomena. Now the cause of animal protection was transformed from reformist calls for animal protection into radical calls for societal redemption. Here it is quite important to understand the difference between animal rights and animal welfare. The proponents of animal welfare seek to alleviate the suffering of animals while attempting to question the fundamental basis of whether it is acceptable to exploit animals in the first place, while the proponents of animal rights reject the idea that animals had to have a value to the human species in order to be deserving of rights. However, a person can work for animal welfare as well as animal rights.

Whereas the 19th century movement focused upon experimental dissection of animals and mistreatment of companion animals, the contemporary animal rights movement has evolved to question virtually all forrns of animal utilization and control. Like its Victorian predecessor, the animal rights movement has used publicity, exposes and apocalyptic literature to frame the issues surrounding the state of animals in moralistic terms.

However, unlike its progenitor the radical animal rights movement extends rights-based claims for moral consideration and legal protection to animals. Millions of animals every year are used in schools and universities for educational purposes. Many of these animal studies are not experiments at all, but simply a sort of demonstration and there is little objective evidence that manipulative exercises on live animals are necessary for educational purposes. One of the greatest cruelties in medical research is the deliberate infliction of burns on animals. Vivisection of animals should be stopped so that animals no longer suffer and die in laboratory experiments. Animal experimentation plays a predominant role in psychological research. Countless animals have been sacrificially dismembered, drugged, starved, fatigued, frozen, electrically shocked, infected, cross-bred, maddened and killed in the belief that their behaviour closely observed, would cast light on the nature of human kind.

The Animal rights movement's claim to moral equivalence between humans and animals originates in two opposing philosophical schools—Utilitarianism and Moral Rights. The utilitarian argument points out that ethical decisions are dependent on their utility, stating that ethical decisions should maximise pleasure while minimising pain. It cites the utilitarian creed—the greatest good for the greatest number for the longest time—as its justification. Animal liberationists argue that since animals and people both feel pain and pleasure, the utilitarian creed should be expanded to include animals. In other words, they argue that the interests of animals should be equivalent to those of humans in determining ethical decisions. Extending the evaluation of utility from humans to animals can be traced to school of utilitarian Oxford philosophers originating during the 1960's and the 1970's. Finding its most popularized expression in Peter Singer's *Animal Liberation* (1975), the utilitarian justification for moral consideration of animal is considered seminal to the movement's current growth.

Whereas the utilitarian justifications rely on the utility of moral extensionism, the rights argument emphasizes similarities in the physiology, and therefore the inherent value, between higher mammals. Rights based philosophers consider utilitarian moral considerations of animals to be flawed in tow aspects. First, utilitarianism is based on the assumption that types of pains and pleasures are qualitatively different, and second, utilitarianism allows the exploitation of animals if it is deemed necessary for the greater good. In response to utilitarianism's situational protection of animals, Tom Regan, an animal rights philosopher advocates a rights-based approach. He believes that rights are dichotomous and absolute, thus extending protection under all circumstances. He argues that since animals have consciousness expectations, and desires, they likewise have personal autonomy. He states that "unless or until we are shown that there are better reasons for denying that these animals have beliefs and desires, we are rationally entitled to believe that they do." He attempts to protect their expectations and desires by granting personal autonomy through the extension of moral claims. Differentiating between moral and legal rights, he states that legal rights are provided to enfranchised citizens and consist of valid claims that have correlative duties. In his tension of moral rights to animals, however, Tom Regan argues that social justice calls for respectful treatment of all beings who have inherent value.

Each school of thought has produced potent political and social critics of animal exploitation. The animal rights movement consists of various organisations which can be subdivided into roughly three categories. According to James Jasper and Dorothy Nelkin in their book *The Animal Rights Crusade* (1992) these groups are, the welfarists, the pragmatists and the fundamentalists. Welfarists believe that animals are objects of compassion, deserving protection and that there are some boundaries between species. Their goals include avoiding animal cruelty, limiting animal populations and adopting animals. Welfarists' strategies include reformist legislation and human education, animal shelters and animal birth control programmes, and cooperation with existing agencies. The pragmatists believe that animals deserve moral and legal consideration with a balance between human and animal interests and that there is some hierarchy of animals. Their explicit goals include elimination of all unnecessary suffering by reducing and replacing existing uses of animals and their strategies include protests and debates, pragmatic cooperation, negotiation and acceptance of short term compromises. The fundamentalists argue that animals have absolute moral and legal rights to personal autonomy and self-determination, with equal rights across species, especially among higher vertebrates. They seek total and immediate abolition of all animal exploitation and use moralistic rhetoric and public condemnation in conjunction with civil disobedience and direct actions to protest the use of animals.

Each of these groups is composed of dedicated activists who believe firmly in the morality of their causes. Yet who are the activists? While the animal rights movement is not monolithic, its activists tend to fit a uniform demographic profile. Social science data indicate that activists tend to be higher educated, middle aged, middle class caucasian females from urban areas with the inclination and the political will to effect change. Although most political activists are portrayed as ignorant socially marginal individuals who are overly emotional about animals, what emerges from the data is a composite of a movement that is broad based and politically sophisticated and of activists who are neither ignorant nor marginal. Indeed, animal rights activists are motivated by moralistic concerns rather than scientific, economic or leisure-use justification for animal exploitation.

Thus, in the 1960's the philosophical ground work had been done for a radical reinterpretation of the way people treated animals. Whereas people had traditionally viewed animals as objects to be used, albeit within some form of highly personal, existential moral constraint, the animal rights movement argued that animals have personal autonomy and moral agencies and therefore should be protected from human exploitation through the provision of rights. Because of transformation of animals into objects of commodities production and profit extraction, the alienation and objection of animals has reached its zenith. The treatment of animals as objects is intimately connected with the view deeply entrenched in western culture and its discourses of a sharp discontinuity between animals and humans. This picture dictates that human as subjects, live in a world of culture, agency and freedom while animals, as objects, inhabit a realm of necessity passivity and compulsion.

Barbara Noske (1989) criticizes the predominant image of the animal as an object in Western science and thought and the treatment of animals as objects, particularly in animal industries. She objects to reductionist models of the animal in both natural and social sciences as constructs that support utilitarian attitudes with respect to the treatment of animals. Donald R. Griffin (1992) challenges the stronghold against animal mentality in the behavioural sciences. He brings together a formidable collection of findings from the study of behaviour arguing compellingly that animals experience conscious thoughts and feelings.

Human have treated animals as cogs in the human-centered ecosystems : economic resources, commodities and means of production for human use. Apart from functioning as subsistence factors, animals have also been made to serve non-subsistence human purposes, for instance as objects of prestige or sacrifice or as totems. Animals in this capacity have been vested with religious significance and with symbolic and metaphorical power. In addition, historians have focused on the roles that animals play in human ceremonial and religious life. However, interest in animal totems or animal symbols is no guarantee against an anthropocentric approach. More often than not, such interest serves as an excuse to stop at human constructs instead of paying attention to animals themselves. Scholars in the humanities generally assume that sociality and culture do not exist outside the human realm. These phenomena are taken to be exclusively human, a view which lands anthropologists and their colleagues in the circular argument that animals, not being human, cannot possibly be social or cultural beings. Social scientists characterize humans in terms of material and social arrangements these humans make and by which they are also shaped : as beings who socially constitute and are constituted.

Millions of animals every year are used in schools and universities for educational purposes. Many of these animal studies are not experiments at all, but simply demonstrations, and there is little objective evidence that manipulative exercises on live animals are necessary for educational purposes. One of the greatest cruelties in medical research is the deliberate infliction of burns on animals. With so many tragic cases of burns victims in the wards of hospitals around the world, it seems totally unnecessary to inflict such suffering on sentient animals. Vivisection should be stopped so that animals no longer suffer and die in laboratory experiments. The scientists would have no introduce better and safer methods of research so we would all be better off.

If zoo visitors were made aware of the suffering of the animals, most of the zoos in India and the world over would be demolished and the animals liberated by a compassionate humanity. The zoo scientists have too little knowledge to breed successfully many of the endangered species. Sanctuaries are better places for breading where natural habitat can be provided to them. Also, natural habitats preserve much more than a single species.

"Fashionable cruelties" were often practised upon animals

who liked to have their flesh cooked alive in a certain way by the smart landaus, phactons, and victories of the well-to-do classes. Progress in humane feelings is hard to discern during our times when half a dozen cows die daily on the street of Delhi.

Social scientists tend to treat our continuity with animals as a purely material residue from a pre-historical past. At the most our "animalness" (our body) is taken to have formed the material base upon which our real "humanness" (mind, sociality, culture, language) could arise. Our humanness is built on an animal basis of sorts, with a vital addition.

The social scientific image of animals and animalness has been shaped by science which is often denounced as reductionism and objectifying. Such reductionism is denounced, however, only when directed at human beings. Natural sciences, particularly the bio-behavioral sciences, are responsible for creating the current animal image. The bio-behavioral scientific characterization of animals is presented in terms of observable traits and mechanisms thought to be encoded in the animal's genetic make-up. Unlike genetic transmission, human cultural transmission does not pass over the heads of the individuals concerned. It involves the active if not always conscious participation of the transmitters (the teachers) as well as that of the recipients (the learners). It is not as if the former are active and the latter passive.

However, there are some courageous animal scientists who do say that animals are more human-like and less object-like than their own science will have us believe. But they often say such things off the record or rather apologetically. This is understandable since they are committing a sacrilege both from the perspective of the animal sciences and from that of the human sciences. Those scientists who have actually studied animals as participant observers, the common anthropological approach to human societies, reveal a tension in their writings between the accepted biological codes and their own experiences with animal personhood. Jane Goodall, who is working with chimpanzees, Dian Fossey who lived and died among mountain gorillas, the Douglas-Hamilton couple and Cynthia Moss who are living and working among elephants, all write about touching experiences with animal personhood. Their science cannot handle these forms of animal reality and tends to belittle or ignore them. The animal sciences are simply not equipped to deal with those characteristics in animals which according to the social sciences make humans human.

As Donald R. Griffin, the founder of cognitive ethology, has suggested, animals can think about finding food, escaping from predators, capturing prey, constructing artefacts (such as bird nests of the dams of beavers), or making and using tools. Having goals or purposes is likely to involve thinking, as are communicating activities (such as bird songs and primate calls) and complex social interactions. These interactions may entail one animal anticipating what another is likely to do next, or deceiving or manipulating other animals in a social group. Scientists usually study these cognitive activities in an animals's natural environment or in semi-natural captive conditions. The basic underlying processes, include learning, memory, problem solving, and decision making. Astounding memories are possessed by some animals, notably squirrels and certain birds, which may hide thousands of food items in the fall to be recovered during the winter. Evidence indicates that in winter such animals do remember specific hiding spots and are not merely looking in likely places. Certain phenomena seem particularly revealing of animal cognition. Spatial knowledge suggesting the use of a cognitive map, for example, is employed by very small-brained creatures such as the honeybee, and certain coral reef fish create and remember routes between feeding areas and protected night time resting places. In the realm of tool use, chimpanzees in the wild have been observed to store particular stones that they use to smash open hard nuts. The stones are stored in specific locations, and the apes go to the closest stone appropriate to the size of a chosen nut. As more effective procedure, some chimpanzees use a solid rock surface beneath the nut as an "anvil," while others also employ a "wedge" to prop up the anvil. Apes, dolphins, sea lions, and parrots have been known to have exhibited simple numeric abilities up to about the numbers 6 or 7. Some of them have shown, as well, an ability to add small numbers of items. Some apes, and parrots, have also achieved "meat-cognition," describing the colour and shape of objects when asked as well as "naming" or at least labelling them. And pigeons can correctly discriminate between instances of categories such as flower, chair, and cat.

The view of animals as non-feeling creatures of reflex, as exemplified by Rene Descartes's philosophy of science in the 17th century, has long since been undercut by other philosophical approaches and by better understanding of evolution and animal behaviour. Its effects are still observable, however, in some of the ways in which animals are used today, despite the efforts of numerous humane organisations. Animal-rights activists have sought, with some success, to obtain better control over the use of animals in laboratories for scientific research and the testing of products. A number of activists would eventually ban such use altogether and would also promote the practice of vegetarianism.

Animal rights is the philosophy of allowing animals to have the most basic rights that all sentient beings desire; the freedom to live a natural life free from human exploitation, unnecessary pain and suffering, and premature death. This is what the animal rights movement is all about; it is not about working for equality between human and animals. The concept of animal rights has come to play an important role in several areas of concern over human treatment of other animals. These areas range from hunting and trapping of animals, to obvious cases of mistreatment of work or sport animals or pets, to less apparent cases such as the widely accepted practices of animal experimentation for scientific purposes and factory farming. Concern further extends to broad ecological issues of human responsibility for the Earth's environment and the threat of extinction to many endangered species.

The question as to whether animals have any inherent rights or not has often been raised in religion and philosophy. The Judeo-Christian thought places humanity at the centre of creation and all the other forms of life are treated as subservient to human needs and desires. As compared to this, Buddhism emphasizes the unity of begins where all forms of life are considered sacred and are therefore not to be injured.

The Buddha paid special attention to the important task of building up an ethical system in which justice for animals is regarded as the norm rather than the exception. Animals in Buddhism are capable of both passion and voluntary motion and so are not simply driven out by impulses beyond their control. The Buddha's frequent reference to the migration of *samskārās* and rebirth across species reduces the psychic space between humans and other beings. If man really believes that he is higher in ethics and spirituality than other creatures then he must stop living by standards that are lower than those of the vulture or the hyena.

Animals, like young children and some mentally handicapped people, do not have the intellectual capacity to understand what rights are. They are therefore unable to consciously respect or abuse the rights of others. However, this does not give us an excuse or right to abuse them. They remain individuals capable of suffering, so we must respect their rights even if they are incapable of respecting ours. Nobody is completely harmless. It is impossible to live your life without causing some harm. We all accidentally tread on ants or breathe in flies. But the Buddha's concern was about causing harm deliberately and unnecessarily, something most of us can easily avoid.

The physical mechanisms for feeling pain are the same throughout the higher animals. Pain whether you be a bird, a fish, a mouse or a human. But in some respects human suffering can differ from that of other animals. For example, a human being in prison for a short term can take comfort in knowing that his sentence will soon be served, whereas a captive animal knows only the agony of being trapped. On the other hand, a captive animal cannot suffer from the knowledge that it will be executed at dawn. Sometimes we do suffer to a greater degree than other animals, sometimes theirs is the greater suffering.

The ability to reason is not unique to humans. It is a function of the forebrain, one of the three basic functions present in all vertebrates. It varies in complexity from fish to the higher mammals. In human beings it is very highly developed but that is a difference of degree, not of kind. We have an arrogant tendency to describe our actions as products of reason but the same actions in other animals as products of instinct. Where do you draw the line? It is not always easy to "draw the line", for example, at what point does a person become old or happy or clever?, it's impossible to say, and yet we know people who definitely are old or happy or clever. In the same way, nobody knows at precisely what level or complexity an animal becomes capable of suffering. It doesn't really matter where the line actually falls. A person who truly strives to live without cruelty will have pushed the line back as far as he can. Nobody can do more than that. Animals, like young children and some mentally handicapped people, do not have the intellectual capacity to understand what rights are. They are therefore unable to consciously respect or abuse the rights of others. However, this does not give us an excuse or right to abuse them. They remain individuals capable of suffering, so we must respect their rights even if they are incapable of respecting ours.

It is also important to understand the difference between Animal Rights and Animal Welfare. Proponents of animal welfare seek to alleviate the suffering of animals while they are being exploited, without attempting to question the fundamental basis of whether it is acceptable to exploit animals in the first place. Supporters of animal rights reject the idea that animals need to have a value to the human species in order to be deserving of rights. However, a person can work for both animal welfare and animal rights.

This crusade has persuasively made moral issues of hunting, industrial testing of cosmetics, drugs and toilertries, factory farming, humane slaughter, and fur production (both wild and ranch). Pit bull and cock fighting have now expanded to rodeos, circuses, Hollywood films, zoos, and animal shows, with only partial impact.

Jasper and Nelkin present an overview of the evolution of the animal rights movement by dividing the movement into three parts : (i) Since the 1860s, the original SPCA "welfarists" were part of a larger humanitarian tradition of helping others; (ii) Since the 1970s, more assertive "pragmatists" like Henry Spira have demanded "animal rights" using stronger methods in order to force negotiations with those who violate these rights; (iii) Since the 1980s, "fundamentalists" like People for Ethical Treatment of Animals (PETA) have sought to protect animal rights without "hobnobbing in the halls with our enemy"[10] or compromising. Even in the 1990s, welfarist groups like the HSUS and SPCA remain the largest in both membership and funding. Yet there has been a meteoric rise of the crusader factions, eclipsing the welfarists; pragmatists like Spira's Animal Rights International, Joyce Tischler's Animal Legal Defence Fund, Cleveland Amory's Fund for Animals, as well as fundamentalists like PETA, Trans Species Unlimited, and Animal Liberation Front. Moreover, the achievements of the crusader groups are telling. For instance, PEETA grew from its two founders in 1980 to 300,000 in 1990,[11] and between 1980-87 much of the cosmetics industry had come to pledge an end to all animal testing and allocated $ 5,000,000 for research on alternatives.[12] Some of this strength comes from an alliance with parallel movements against pollution, racism, sexism, nuclearism, agribusiness, even cholesterol.

Animal rights activists like Peter Singer believe that animals should be guaranteed certain rights by law like the humans. They believe that animals have three basic rights :

1. Each species has the right to express the natural behaviour of its kind : Every animal has behaviour that is natural to it. For example, calves have an urge to chew their cud, partially digested grass or hay. Chickens need to peck and scratch for their food. Animal rights advocates want to stop any human practice, such as feeding veal calves only liquid formula or raising chickens in cages high above the ground, that interferes with these behaviours.

2. All animals have the right to a natural life span without suffering neglect or cruelty : Current animal welfare laws protect many animals from neglect and cruelty. Animal rights advocates want to expand the definition of cruelty to include fear, suffering, or early death caused by humans. This is perhaps the most controversial idea of all because to respect this right, people must not eat meat, hunt, conduct experiments on animals, or wear clothes made from animal products.

3. Every animal has the right to a humane death : Some activists think animals should not be killed for any reason. These people even oppose the humane killing of animals suffering from incurable diseases. Animal rights advocates do believe, however, that when animals are killed, whether they are put to sleep, slaughtered for food, or killed during scientific experiments, death should be as painless and free of fear as possible.

A person should be punished for being cruel to animals, if he/she —

1. tortures or seriously overworks an animal ;
2. fails unreasonably to provide necessary food, care, or shelter for an animal in his/her custody;
3. abandons unreasonably an animal in his custody;
4. transports or confines an animal in a cruel manner;
5. kills, injures, or administers poison to an animal, other than cattle, horses, sheep, swine, or goats, belonging to another without legal authority or the owner's effective consent;
6. causes one animal to fight with another; or
7. uses a live animal as lure.

Don't eat anything with a face', is the Animal Rights Maxim.

Our intellectual capacity gives us the ability to always win when our interests and those of other species clash, but that does not give us a moral victory. The only quality we have that sets us 'above' other animals is compassion, and compassion forbids that we cause suffering and death of others for our own ends.

The Buddhist tradition is a varied series of religious phenomena and few wild generalizations are possible. Attitude towards other animals, however is one of the few areas where generalizations can be made. Generally the Buddhist tradition was unconcerned with any systematic exploration of the physical world, which accepted most of the views of other animals that were important in the cultures and subcultures where Buddhism prospered.

At its core Buddhism is a salvation — like concern for the individual. Theoretically, each individual Buddhist attempts to discover about himself or herself the basic features of existence experienced by the Buddha. The core of this experience is that each living being has, in the end, no lasting self. Similarly, there is no lasting deity or creator of the earth. Instead, all is in process and subject to change. The unifying elements in the tradition are (i) reverence of some kind for the Buddha and (ii) a strong, consistent hermit-like tradition that adheres to time-honoured rules of conduct. It is this tradition that has provided a relative unity and stability in the moral code of conduct.

Here we are going to discuss the nature of early Buddhist attitude towards animals from the variety of textual sources and folk traditions. The treatment of animals is included in the first Buddhist precept—"*Panatipāta Vermānī*", which means 'I refrain from injury to living things. 'It refers to the Buddhist doctrine of *Ahiṃsā* which has far reaching implications. As an extension, it includes within it such virtues as amity (*mettā*) and compassion (*Karuṇā* or *Anukampā*). It emanates from the belief in the oneness of all forms of life and refers not only to non-killing but to all forms of cruelty, harm and oppression. The Buddha was opposed to Brahmanical sacrifices which entailed killing of and cruelty to animals.[13] A *Jātaka* story puts forth that one single act of *hiṃsā* bears its results in hundreds of births.[14] The Buddhist view point is expressed in these words : "As I am, so are these. As these are, so am I. Thus, identifying himself with others the wise man neither kills nor causes to be killed".[15] A bhikkhu who has received ordinance ought not intentionally to destroy the life of any living being down to a worm or an ant.[16] Non-injury to animals clearly holds a very prominent place in Buddhist traditions. Animals are regarded to be none other than our very selves. The underlying assumption is that each and every human being has experienced wide variety of animal lives in prior incarnation and if one makes a mistake of significant proportion during human life that one will be born as an animal in punishment for wrong doing. One of the greatest acts of wrongdoing that will cause rebirth as an animal is undue harm to an animal or human. Buddhism views animals as sentient beings. Animals are said to have feelings and emotions and to be able to improve themselves, at least in some of the various parables that are cited. In seeing animals as kin, that is, in accepting the theory of repeated births in the form of increasingly or decreasingly spohisticated animals, depending upon one's deeds, the entire kingdom, including humans, becomes an extended family. So, for the Buddhist, this would be unthinkable. To kill is a great infraction against the religious precepts and certainly would result in future suffering.

The Buddhist ideal of non-injury to animals clearly has implications for the use of animals in product testing and medical research and training. The modern world uses animals for these purposes in large numbers. From a Buddhist perspective, this might be seen as analogous to animal sacrifices in Hinduism. In one case, the animals were sacrificed in the name of religion and in the other case, in the name of 'science and knowledge'. In the western world, the public mood has swung increasingly against the abuse of animals in cosmetics testing. There is also some degree of disquiet concerning the use of animals in school biology classes. The use of animals in medical research at least has strong utilitarian arguments in its favour. Buddhist ethics, though, is not generally based on the principle that the ends justify the means. From the Buddhist point of view, it is more certain that killing an animal is wrong than that generating better drugs etc. from experiments is good. If the early Buddhist attitude to meat eating is applied in this area of concern, though, it will be acceptable for a Buddhist to take drugs which others have developed using animal research. From Buddhist point of view, any one prepared to do animal dissections and experimentation on animals has to know and accept the *kamma* of his actions. This would entail trying to do as little *kamma* as possible, using alternative methods if available, killing only if absolutely necessary, treating the being with tender respect and making sure the knowledge is put to good use. To get rid of this type of cruelty and injury inflicted upon animals, one has to follow the traditional Buddhist behaviour by which one has to liberate animals by buying them from the establishments involved in experimentation on animals. It might be argued that animals are needed to protect human beings. The Buddhists do in fact include within their system a provision for committing violence out of self defence.

The Buddhist monastic code (known as the *Vinaya*) reveals that early Buddhists accepted the view that all animals other than humans belong to one realm that is lower than that of human beings. Yet it is clear that Buddhists did not know other animals well despite their claim that all animals, from the simplest of *Kammic* forms up to the most complex ones such as the large-brained social mammals, form a single kingdom that does not include human beings. The tradition displayed poor awareness of the elaborate realities of the lives of other animals, lumping them together in a group below human beings in the hierarchy of the universe.

In one very important way, however, Buddhism was clearly revolutionary with regard to moral significance of other animals, for Buddhism, along with Jainism, was important in opposing the sacrifice of other animals that was part of the Brahmanical tradition in our country. Similarly, the tradition spread important precepts, or moral undertakings, that affirmed that killing other sentient beings was a violation of the most basic moral norms of the universe. The first precept in the tradition is," I undertake to abstain from the destruction of life." This is an ethical commitment that the tradition from its very beginnings has identified as part of the case of religious living. Society for a Buddhist, then, is not taken in a narrow sense of human society, but in a broader sense of a community comprising all living or sentient beings.

There is another, less favourable side to the Buddhist view of other animals, however. The way in which early Buddhists talked about other animals reveals that they thought about them in rather negative ways. For Buddhists, any animal other than a human being was in an inferior position and could, if it lived a perfect life, be born as a human being. This reliance on reincarnation as an explanation of the justice of the present state of any being also functioned as a justification of many of the social divisions. Rich human beings were deemed to have been rewarded for past good deeds and lame, stupid, and unfortunate human beings were deemed to be paying for part bad deeds. Below even the most unfortunate and morally corrupt human beings were all other animals.

The Buddhist attitude towards use of other animals reveals these same hierarchical notions of life. Elephants, whose natural history was poorly known to Buddhists, were used with Buddhist approval. Indeed, the Buddha himself understood that the use of elephants was a morally justified reward. Rich human beings were entitled to ride around on elephants, having lived past lives in such a way as to justly deserve this reward. Sadly, the Buddhist scriptures contain many indications that elephants suffered during captivity, being deprived of their naturally complex social lives with other elephants. The Buddha can be deemed as the greatest of all humanity, and his path, the most sensitive of all paths leading to the reduction of human agonies of all kinds. Buddhism insists on self-reliance and teaches people to pursue knowledge and practise essential virtues, such as friendship, compassion, non-violence, love and service to human beings and also non-human beings. It can also be considered as a form of religion without any complicated and unintelligible rituals. It suggests a way to conceive the fundamental unity of all beings and provide an effective expression for such a feeling so that humanity has a common bond and a common end.

The Buddha preached the view of equal sanctity of beings which is his most important teaching. In his teachings he solicited : "O, sorrowless enlightened one, you behold those glorious beings, and show the path of getting rid of all miseries and sorrow".[17] Buddhisms is a doctrine of mass benediction preached by the Buddha. The Eight Fold Path taught by the Buddha stresses Right Livelihood (*Sammajiva*) which means abstaining from a livelihood that brings harm to other beings, intoxication, deceit, treachery, sooth saying etc.[18] Buddhism emphasized equal sanctity of all beings. It has preached about humanity, universal love, and abstaining from harming fellow beings and non-human beings. Citing the example of an mother, the Buddha said," As she would be very good towards her only child, her well-beloved son, so ye too should be very good towards all creatures everywhere and every on".[19]

Buddhism, the interpreter of non-violence doctrine, denotes very clearly how and why man should not indulge in violence or harming other beings because," All are afraid of the rod (punishment), all fear death. Taking oneself as the example, one shall not strike, shall not let strike. One who strikes with a rod beings that are longing for happiness, if such a person seeks happiness, will not secure happiness after death. One who does not strike with a rod beings that are longing for happiness, such a person will secure happiness after death. Speak not any harsh word, if spoken to, he may speak it back".[20]

In a discussion, the Buddha and Kutādanta brahmana (*Tathāgata* by an instance) have preached a non-violence doctrine saying that religious sacrifices may not be performed with the act of slaughter, as king Malavijītā did in Pauranika-age. Further, the narrated, "No slaughter of cows took place, neither of the nanny goats nor of the sheep and no other animals were killed. Not to say of living beings, no act of cutting trees was done in order to erect the post (*Yupa stambha*) for ablation performance".[21]

Thus, the whole analysis and understanding of the Buddhist Philosophy helps us to have a clearer understanding of the present situation prevalent in the world. In the *Mettā-Sutta* a prayer is offered in the following words : "As the mother protects her child even at the risk of her own life, so that there be mutual protection and goodwill limitless among all beings, let limitless goodwill prevail in the whole world above, below and around, untarnished with any feeling of disharmony and discord".[22] With a right understanding of one's existence among all, avoiding being cruel to other living creatures, not exploiting beyond the limit of one's survival and right aspiration and right conduct, most of the problems related with animals or non-human beings of today can be solved. The teachings of Buddhism have concentrated on the theory of *kamma* and the theory of cause and effect and demonstrate that unmindful neglect of these principles of right living may tend to chaos resulting in aggressive attitude towards animals.

Religion, one of whose tenets traditionally has been reverence for life (including respect for animals and the earth), is one of the strongest and most influential institutions in our society, and is a guiding force for hundreds of millions of people. What an impact organized religion can have when it embraces concern for all animals! Yet what is preached often may not be what is practised. Buddhism has particularly extolled the virtues of compassion and mercy. The Buddha fervently argued the rights of other-than-human beings and the importance of making ethical treatment of all animals a theological priority. This is a powerful and significant heritage.

Animals figure as central characters and our treatment, exploitation and killing of them is powerfully questioned. *Udānavagga*, a Buddhist text, is of the view that, "When a man has pity on all living creatures then only is he noble. Hurt not others with that which pains yourself." Again in *Vinaya of Cullavagga Khandhaka* it is written that, "The Buddha has mercy even on the meanest thing." Once Again we find compassionate note towards animals in another Buddhist text named *Mahāvagga* which is as follows :

"All beings seek for happiness; so let your compassion extend itself to all." In *Dhammapada*, the Buddha is of the view that, "Because he has pity on every living creature, therefore is a man called 'holy'."

An astonishing variety of animal emotions are expressed through the differnet *Jātaka* stories. For instance, when asked why Alex, the gray parrot, learned so much more than thousands of pet parrots over the centuries, his trainer ascribes the bird's success to "the model/rival method," a system whereby the animal sees another student being praised for learning, and presumably competes for affection. Other examples suggest that animals may blush, wage war, exact revenge, tell stories and experience beauty. In the authors' view, much of this behaviour surpasses what is necessary for survival. There is evidence of every sort of behaviour among animals, from rage to jealousy to altruism to romantic love, and they have assumed that if an animal behaves as if it is feeling a particular emotion, then one can usefully describe that emotion in human terms. Animals feel pain and sorrow and all the other emotions; these feelings cannot be ignored in our behaviour towards them. A hare is not going to paint Leonarda Da Vinci's Mona Lisa, but then neither is our next door neighbour. We do not for this reason conclude that we have the freedom to experiment upon him, hunt him for sport, or eat him for food.

The Buddha showed a new path to humans to take a new step towards a new vision of a humane planetary stewardship which will become a reality only if we begin to make right choices now, based upon the ethic of respect and reverence for all life and upon *ahiṃsā*. Our attitude based upon the principles of *Mettā, Karunā* and *Ahiṃsā* will do much to heal the planet and ourselves in the process. We do not own the land; it is entrusted to us for the future children of the Earth.

The human view of the animal world has been ambivalent, a knife-edge balancing of fear with fascination, affection with exploitation, kindness with cruelty, complicated by theological explanations of the universe and clouded by self-deceit. It is also interesting. But even more interesting would be the animals's point of view. That unfortunately is not available. However, if we were to go by what the different animal-*Bodhisattvas* as feel, surely it would feel quite embarrassing to be a human. We do, however, know this : animals have been largely at the disposal of the human-animal since he evolved into a cunning, predatory overlord of the creatures of the earth, the only vertebrate that freedly chooses to torture or kill all forms of sentient life and is able to do it.

Equality of consideration (Buddhism talks about it) : Our present attitudes are based on a long history of prejudice and arbitrary discriminations. There can be no reason except the selfish desire to preserve the privileges of the exploiting group for refusing to extend the basic principle of equality of consideration to members of other species.

The basic principle of equality does not require equal or identical treatment; it requires equal consideration. This means that our concern for others and our readiness to consider to consider their interests ought not to depend on what they are like or on what abilities they may possess. Just as we are concerned about a child to learn to read and write, concern for the well-being of a pig may require no more than that we leave him alone with other pigs in a place where there is adequate food and room to run freely. The basic element of taking into consideration the interests of the being, whatever those interests may be, must be extended to all beings-black or white, male or female, human or non-human.

The capacity for suffering, or more strictly suffering and / or enjoyment or happiness, is the vital characteristic that gives a being the right to equal consideration. The Buddha talked exactly the same. The capacity for suffering and enjoyment is a prerequisite for having interests at all, a condition that must be satisfied before we can speak of interests in a meaningful way. There can be no excuse for ignoring the suffering of a being. If a being suffers there can be no moral justification for refusing to take that suffering into consideration. If a being is not capable of suffering, or of experiencing enjoyment or happiness, there is nothing to be taken into consideration. So the limit of sentience (capacity to suffer and/or experience enjoyment) is the only defensible boundary of concern for the interests of others.

Buddhist texts are replete with examples where animals are cared for. In Buddhism, love for animals is not sentimentality but true spirituality. Buddhism is scrupulous even in the smallest matters where either life or well-being of beings are concerned. The Buddha found a profound rapport with all living things. Buddhism believes in the spiritual unity of all creatures. It exhorts humans to befriend them. We have obligations to animals to care for them.

Factory farming is quite a common phenomenon in the modern world. Buddhism is against unnatural production of this kind. Buddhism is against keeping pet animals. It restricts their freedom by uprooting them from their natural environment. Human morality must expand to acknowledge and respect the rights of non-human animals. If human animals have rights, such as the right to life, so do non-human animals. To prevent most of today's suffering by animals would require "radical changes in our treatment of animals that would involve our diet, the farming methods we use, experimental procedures in many fields of science, our approach to wildlife and to hunting, trapping and the wearing of furs, and areas of entertainment like circuses, rodeos, and zoos." Most animals are aware of their environment, have beliefs and desires, possess memory and expectations about the future, and are able to act intentionally in seeking to fulfil their desires or purposes. Animals are harmed by suffering pain and also by being deprived of the pleasures of life. e.g., by being confined in zoos, cages etc. An animal's untimely death is also a deprivation, one of the most fundamental and irreversible kind. Tom Regan gives the example of four humans and a dog in a boat that can hold only four. Tom Regan agrees that most people would choose to throw the dog overboard on the ground that the *magnitude of the harm* done to each being in the life boat must be weighed. Writes Regan, "No reasonable person would deny that the death of any of the four humans would be a greater loss, and thus a greater harm, than would be true in the case of the dog."

REFERENCES

1. Barbara Noske, 1969, p. 40
2. Passmore, John (1975), 'The Treatment of animals,' Journal of the history of ideas, 36, p. 195-218.
3. Hume, David (1964)—*The Philosophical Works*, Vol. IV, p. 185.
4. Kant. I, *'Die Metaphysic der sitten'* (1956) vol. IV, p. 578-9.
5. Bentham, J. (1760), Introduction to Principle of Morals and Legislation.
6. Dietler, W. (1787) Gerechtigkeit gegen. Thiere. Mainz: schillersdrem verlge, p. 28.
7. Hommel, Karl F. (1782-7) Rhapsodia questionum in foro questiatic abententum negne arren logibus decisarum, Vol. II, p. 39, ed. Karl G. Roessing.
8. Ibid.
9. Passmore, John, op. cit. p. 209 (1975)
10. James, Japser and Dorothy Nelkin. *'The Animal Rights Crusade : The Growth of a Moral Protest.* New York : The Free Press, p. 154.
11. Ibid., p. 31.
12. Ibid., p. 2.
13. See *Kutadanta Sutta* in *Digha Nikāya* : GS. II, 42-43, Ibid., IV, 42-45.
14. *Matakābhata Jātaka* : J.I. 53.
15. H. Saddhatissa, *Buddhist Ethics*, p. 89.
16. Lambert Schmithausen, *Buddhism and Nature*, (1941), p. 4-10.
17. Buddhist dictionary : Nayantilok, p. 81.
18. Rhys Davids, *Psalms of the Brotheren*, 1.33.33
19. Bhikkshu, J.K., *Dhammapada : Dandavaga*, Patna, BSPPB, 1959, p. 129-133.
20. Bhikkhu, J.K., *Suttinipātā : Vasittasutta*, (Patna, BSPPB, 1959), 1959), p. 206-9.
21. Bhikkhu, J.K., *Mettā-sutta* : (Patna, BSPPB, 1959), 8; 149-150.
22. Bhikku, J.K., *'Mettā Sutta* (Patna, BSPPB, 1959), 8; p. 149-50.

Chapter-5

ATTITUDE TOWARDS ANIMALS IN OTHER RELIGIONS

Attitude towards animals can only be determined indirectly from the traces of cultural practices, art, and artefacts that have survived in the archaeological records. Direct comparisons with recent or current cultures are only appropriate where obvious similarities in animal related attitudes, beliefs and values seems to exist.

The idea that animals are fully conscious beings who posses, spiritual power is widespread among all religious traditions and societies. It appears to engender considerable anxiety and guilt about killing animals for food. Most of the these religious traditions and cultures engage in complex rituals and taboos designed either to relieve the guilt arising from killing or to honour the spirit of deceased animals. These are largely based on erroneous understanding of different religious traditions. Failure to treat the animal with appropriate ritual, respect is thought to invite spiritual anger in the form of accidents, ill health or loss of success in future hunting. Most likely or probably, prehistoric hunters must have shared the same attitude towards animals.

Anna Sewel, in her book *Black Beauty* writes that there is no religion without love and people may talk as much as they like about their religion but if it does not teach them to be good and kind to other animals as well as humans, it is a shame". Religion, one of whose tenets traditionally has been reverence for life (including respect for animals and the earth), is one of the strongest and most influential institutions in our society, and is a binding force for hundreds of millions of people. What an impact organized religion can have when it embraces concern for all animals! Yet what is preached often may not be what is practised. Animal theology relates Christian thinking to contemporary debates about the status and rights of the animals and seeks to address and redress the failure of historical theology to take seriously alternative in sights that are largely silent Christian traditions. Systematic in sights that are largely silent in Christian traditions. Systematic theology largely proceeded on the basis of virtual non-existence of animals. Historically, animals have been the outcastes of theology, defined as beings with no mind, reason, immortal soul or moral status. The question raised by animal theology is whether Christian doctrine is necessarily speciesist and whether it can incorporate animal-centred concerns into mainstream thinking.

In terms of the traditional doctrine, there are three main areas of concern. The first is creation. Much theological emphasis has been laid on the special creation of humans to the detriment of the non-humans i.e. animals. But the "specialness" of humans in creation can be read in another way : as support for the special role of humanity in looking after the world, not as the master but as the servant species. The second is incarnation. The traditional doctrine affirms that God became human in the person of Jesus Christ. While this is frequently taken as a vindication of human uniqueness, some church fathers have argued that the incarnation is the raising up of all fleshy substance to be with God. The word 'flesh' affirms all flesh, animal and human. The third is redemption. While much traditional interpretation excludes animals directly or indirectly from the sphere of God's redemptive purposes, it can be argued that notions of ultimate justice specifically require animal immortality.

As far as Animal theology is concerned, it is quite clear from the discussion that animals have occupied a very prominent place in our mind and due to this one could find a place for the animals in religious texts.

Christian Attitude Towards Animals

Many of the important ideas that have governed our

understanding and treatment of animals arise from Christian and Jewish sources or from reaction to, development of, or opposition to them. Many zoophiles, meaning animal lovers or those who care for animals, maintain that Christian indifference has been one of the main causes for the low status of animals. Within the Christian tradition in almost every period of history, there were both strong negative and positive ideas and attitudes towards animals. Though it is true that largely negative ideas have predominated, it would be wrong to suppose that subtradition have not sustained alternative viewpoints and some times radical ones.

There are three major negative tendencies found in the Christian tradition. The first may be called Instrumentalism, the view that animals are here for human use. St. Thomas Acquinas, interpreting Aristotle, held that in the created hierarchy that God had made, animals were intellectually inferior to humans and were made essentially for human use. According to this view, the purpose of animals was primarily, if not exclusively, the service of human subjects. The Second and allied to instrumentalism has been a consistent humanocentricity that has effectively defined animals out of the moral picture. This has been achieved largely through the emphasis upon certain perceived differences between humans and animals. Animals are judged as beings with no reason or immortal soul and incapable of friendship with human subjects. From this it has been deduced that humans have no direct duties to animals because they are not moral subjects of worth in themselves. Many contemporary secular theories, for example contractualism, owe their origin to this developing scholastic view that animals do not form part of moral community with human beings. The third tendency may be described as dualism, the way western culture has made distinctions and separations between, for example, the rational and the non-rational, flesh and spirit, and mind & matter. Animals are still viewed as being on the wrong side of these desirable attributes, the most important of which has been rationality. As scholastic philosophy and theology began to stress the centrality of rational intellect, it followed that animals had no moral status.

Rationality became and in many ways still is, the key to moral significance.

But in order to see the broader picture, we need to set alongside these negative tendencies a range of positive in sights, many of which are clearly biblical in origin. Three important ones of them are presented here. The first centres on the notion of "dominion" found in Genesis 1:28. Although dominion has often been interpreted as little less than tyranny, in the original context it meant that humans had a God given responsibility to care for the earth. A rival interpretation of dominion as "stewardship" or "responsibility" can be traced back to the earliest Christian writers and came to the fore in the emergence of the 18th to 19th century zoophily. The second concerns the notion of 'convenient' found in Genesis-9. Against the prevailing notion that humans and animals are utterly separate, the idea of God's convenant with all living creatures kept alive the sense of a wider kinship. The third positive insight is preserved in the notion of moral generosity, which came to prominence with the emergence of humanitarian movements of the 19th century. By this perspective, we owe animals charity, benevolence and merciful treatment. Cruelty was judged incompatible with Christian discipleship. To act cruelly or even to kill wantonly, was in general, a sign of ingratitude to the Creator. The Christian tradition, which had in many ways supported, defended and provided the ideological justification for the abuse of animals in previous centuries, also came to spearhead a new movement for animal protection in the 20th century.

In Christian texts, it is found that the Old Testament ethics admonish that the land and the cattle which are in the service of man are to be treated as those that have their own intrinsic value and unique destiny which should not be disturbed at any cost. All creations both animate and inanimate are to be treated as our fellow creatures and members in the community to which all human beings belong. A famous Christian saint named Francis of Asisi was known for addressing animals as his brothers and sisters. The legend holds that Francis preached to the wild animals and often talked to the birds in solitude. The Bible recognizes the intrinsic right of all living beings and creatures to exist and fulfil their role within the cosmic community. All living beings have a right to be fruitful and multiply their kind and all of them have a rightful claim on natural resources and human beings have no right to prevent them from this claim.

In this contemporary world, people are beginning to talk about animal rights on par with human rights and now it is being conceived and articulated as a rightful demand. Although Christian scriptures do not explicitly articulate or advocate animal rights, the essence of it in some shape can be found in cultic observances like *Sabbath Day* and *Sabbath Year*. Biblical ethics recognizes the rights of animals and offers them the same treatment meted out to human labour. The Bible also recognizes the rights of animals domesticated for farm labour. All farm animals are to be given proper human treatment. Not only farm animals, but also wild animals are to be assured humane treatment in Christian texts. These prescriptions for the treatment of animals laid down thousands of years ago are truly incredible and have no parallel in any other religion. So, these prescriptions, which were laid down to protect animals from cruelty and mistreatment meted out to them by human beings, show that Christianity can also play a vital role in protecting and changing human attitude towards animals.

Attitude Towards Animals in Hinduism

Hinduism is not a religion in the formal western sense of the term. There is no single founder, so no accountable time when it started. There is revealed scripture, but no single holy book prescribed. Instead there are innumerable names of sages (*ṛṣis*) and saints through the centuries who contributed to this collective idea called Hinduism, and several philosophical works composed in different ages considered significant enough to become the body of the scriptures.

Hinduism, the oldest of the major religious traditions, is not a single religion but an umbrella under which one finds very different kinds of beliefs. These include among others, *Vaiṣṇavism, Śaivism, Śaktism* and *Tāntricism,* each of which in turn is a complex religious tradition that has many forms of its own. In Hinduism, there is no single view of animals. Different views are dominated by two general beliefs that govern the ways in which other animals are conceived. First, human beings, though recognized to be in a continuum with other animals, are considered the model of what biological life should be. A corollary of this belief is the claim that the status "human" is far above the status of any other animal. The second general belief is that any living being's current position in the cycle of life is determined by the strict law of *Kamma.* Belief in reincarnation is the hallmark of most, though not all, Hindus beliefs. These two beliefs have resulted in other animals being viewed with uncertainty. Positively, other animals have been understood to have souls just as do humans. Negatively, they have been understood to be inferior to any human, a corollary of which is the belief that the existence of other animals must be particularly unhappy, at least compared to human existence.

Regarding the attitude towards animals in Hinduism, we find that animals have always received special attention, care and consideration. Numerous Hindu texts advise that all species should be treated as children. In Hindu mythology and iconography there is close relationship between the various deities who are all different aspects of the same divine power. Each divinity is associated with a particular animal and this lends a special dimension to the animal kingdom.

In addition, according to the *Vaiṣṇava* tradition, the evolution of life on this planet is symbolized by a series of divine incarnations beginning with fish moving through amphibious forms and mammals and then into human incarnations. This view clearly holds that man did not spring fully formed to dominate lesser life forms, but rather evolved out of these forms itself and is therefore integrally linked to the whole creation. This leads necessarily to reverence for animal life. The *Yajurveda* lays down that "no person should kill animals helpful to all. Rather by serving them one should attain happiness".[1] This view was later developed by the great *Jaina Tirthankara*, Lord Mahāvīra, who regenerated the ancient faith that lives down to the present day. The Hindu tradition of reverence for all farms of life represents a powerful tradition which needs to be re-nurtured.

Importantly, humans are by no means considered equal to one another in classical Hinduism, for according to the *Sanātana dharma* men are not born equal. Like other animals they are born into that station in life for which their past *kamma* has fitted them. Inequalities in the social system are not viewed as unjust, rather, they are simply consequences of former lives. A common claim is that those who act morally are assured of good rebirth in higher social strata, while wrong doers are assured of being reborn as outcastes or worse yet, as non-human animals.

Despite all this, the tradition has often exhibited great sensitivity to other animals. In one of the Hindu text it is told that one should treat animals exactly as ones own children. A contemporary Hindu who is an environmental ethicist arrests," All lives, human or non-human, are of equal value and all have the same right to existence".[2] More generally, the economics of village life in our country provides many examples of co-existence with other animals and environmentally sensitive ways of living.

The tradition has vast sources and some do support the view that humans have no special privilege or authority over other creatures but instead have more obligations. This argument relies on the belief that many Hindu deities, such as Rāma and Kṛṣṇa (closely associated with monkeys and cows respectively) have been incarnated as other animals. In addition, the deities worshipped in our country include Ganesha, an elephant-headed god, and Hanumān, the monkey god.

This sensitive side in Hindus' awareness of other animals is often symbolized by the image of sacred cows wandering the streets of the country unmolested and free, yet the realities for animals in Hindu societies have been and continue to be more complicated. The traditional respect for other animals has been affected greatly by economic factors that inhibit transmission of ancient values that encourage respect for animals. Now-a-days, the pace of modern development is leaving behind the strong emphasis that almost all Hindu scriptures place on the notion that benefits can be received by not killing or harming other animals. Thus, while there is throughout in the Hindu tradition a culturally significant sense of the continuity of all life, the already pronounced sense of discontinuity between humans and all other animals threatens to change for the worse.

One important ancient form of tradition was challenged by the Buddhist and the Jaina traditions because it was characterized by a heavy emphasis on animal sacrifice. This practice stemmed from the ancient scriptures known as the Vedas. The Jainas and the Buddhists challenge these sacrifices as cruel and unethical and had a great effect on the later Hindu views of the decency of intentionally sacrificing other animals. *Ahiṃsā* has now become a central feature of the tradition.

Hindus are noted for their respect for and consideration of the natural world.[3] It is considered in Hindu tradition that all existence has been created by the Supreme Being, comes from the Supreme Being, and will return to the Supreme Being, which is an adequate basis for the veneration of the natural world in which man finds himself. Animal worship is rooted in Hindu traditions and as is evident from the relics of Mohenjodaro, some form of animal worship was common. The importance of cattle in Vedic India was not merely economic but animals also fulfilled significantly ritualistic and symbolic roles in the Vedic society. Cow milk and dairy products were used in religious ceremonies and offered as ablutions to gods. Towards the end of the Vedic age, cow dung and *ghee* (clarified butter) were used in religious ceremonies as they were thought to have puficatory effect which became prominent in later days and it is still quite prevalent. Several Hindu gods have animals as their mounts, so those animals are also worshipped along with the associated gods. Some of the gods and their mounts are Durgā-Lion, Brahmā-Wild-goose, Indra-elephant, Ganges-

Rat, Śivā-Bull, Saraswati-Swan, Vishnu-Eagle, Kārtikeya-Peacock, Lakṣhmi-Owl etc. Thus, the animals are not only given respect, but also receive reverence in the Hindu society. These two factors have provided a solid foundation for the doctrine of *Ahiṃsā* against animals.

Killing of animals for food is prohibited in the *Rigveda.* Any person committing such an act is called Yatudhan. Animals are also forbidden from being killed in the *Yajurved* which also states that service to animals is a noble activity : "No person should kill animals helpful to all and by serving them one should obtain heaven".[4] Hindus have a deep faith in the doctrine of non-violence. Almost all the Hindu scriptures place strong emphasis on the notion that God's grace can be had by not killing His creatures or harming His creation. Not eating meat, in Hinduism, is considered both an appropriate conduct and duty. As stated in *Manusmṛti,* eating meat is a great sin which cannot be washed away by performing *Ashwamedhā Yajña* for a period of one hundred years. *Yajñavalkaya Smriti* warns against violence towards animals in one of its *sutras* which is as follows :

> "The wicked person who kills animals,
> which are protected has to live in
> hell fire for the days equal to the
> number of hair on the body of that animal"[5]

By the end of the Vedic and the Upanishadic period, Buddhism and Jainism came into existence and protection of animals was further strengthened by various kings who were practising these religions. These religions which arose more as a protest against orthodoxy and rituals of Hindu religion, continued the precepts of animals protections.

While the Aryan deities were mostly personifications of natural phenomena or heavenly bodies, the indigenous non-Aryan people had rituals of image worship of male and female deities. Several mystical animals had their place in the rituals too. Various animals or birds are associated with particular deities as their vehicles and companions. Together with the deities, the respective animals are worshipped and praised.

In *Chhandogya Upanishad*, we find an important statement regarding the meaning of *ahiṃsā*. He who practises *ahiṃsā* towards all creatures, except at holy places (*tirthā*) does not return to this world again.[6] Here holy place means the place of animal sacrifice. Thus, killing for sacrificial purposes was not considered to be morally wrong in Vedic concept. *Ahiṃsā* used in various sense in vedic texts like Medhatithi commentary on Manu, refers to *ahiṃsā* as non-beating of a student by a teacher.[7] Manu says that throughout one's life a twice born and considerate man should not perform any type of *hiṃsā*, which is not prescribed in the vedas (*aveda-vihita*) even at the time of distress.[8] Manu adds that the *hiṃsā* prescribed in the Vedas should be construed to mean *ahiṃsā* because moral duties spring out from the vedas.[9] Some commentators like Sarvjñanārāyana take *vedic hiṃsā* to include *ahiṃsā* but to Medhātithi, Vedic *hiṃsā* is morally equal to Vedic *ahiṃsā* in the sense that both produce the some result.

This Vedic concept of *ahiṃsā* appears also in the *Mahābhārata* where it is written that the violence done to an evil-doer (*asādhu-hiṃsā*) for maintaining wordly affairs (*lok-yātra*) is *ahiṃsā*.[10] Moreover, killing of animals has vedic sanction in the preparation of *madhuparaka* (a mixture of honey and meat) in the vedic sacrifices and in offerings made to one's forefathers as well as God.[11] This inclusion of vedic *hiṃsā* in the notion of non-violence may be explained by the idea that if God has directed man to do good and evil (*sādhuasādhu*), the moral responsibility for the result goes to God.[12] The vedic conception of *ahiṃsā* is prevalent in the early upanishads in legal literatuare, very frequently also in other *Dharmashāstras, Purāṇas,* in the *Mimāṃsā* school of thought and even in *saṃskāras'* writing.[13]

We have discussed the practices of *ahiṃsā* in the Vedic and Jaina tradtions, we now turn to its mention and some applications in the Hindu or the Brahmanical traditions. In the earliest phase of Hindu traditions, we do not find any emphasis on *ahiṃsā*. It is only in the later phase, the classical form of

Hinduism, that non-violence or *ahiṃsā* is seen as an important value. It may be surmised that this phase of Hinduism, starting from around the 6th century B.C., is marked by a merging of traditions; perhaps Sramanic or proto yogic attitudes and influences from Jainism directly influenced Hindu texts and teachings as they developed. In the *Rigveda,* brāhmans and others eat meat but by the time of classical period, vegetarianism becomes a hallmark of high caste status.

The highest duty according to the Śānti-Parava is to secure the happiness (*Sukha*) of all creatures.[14] The Hindus feel very strongly that animal life ought to be preserved, especially in the case of the cow. In the *Rigveda,* the cow is frequently called *aghanya* which means one not to be killed. According to a Puranic lore, the wicked people who despire the cow do not go upwards.[15]

Hunting (*Mṛgayā*), too, involves some sin even for a *Kṣatriya,* but it is possible to destroy the sin by dedication (*tapas*) and by surrender to God (*Māt-upasraya*).[16] However, according to a story told in *Varāha-Purāna,* a hunter tells a forest-dweller that he himself kills only one animal a day and offers part of the flesh to God and that his offering purifies the killing. However, the other man, engaged in agriculture is said to kill, in the process of accumulating grain, many more living beings in the form of seeds, and he also does not offer anything to God and hence is guilty of *Mahāmāṃsā* or flesh eaten without ritual offerings.[17]

In *Chhandogya Upanishad, ahiṃsā* is mentioned among the list of virtues which are desirable from human beings. "The laws of Manu" played an important role in shaping Hindu society, which list *ahiṃsā* among the rules to be observed by all human beings to protect themselves and also to protect men and animals. But meat-eating is traditionally sanctioned in Hinduism as part of sacrificial process and also in emergency situations such as famine.

The *Mahābhārata,* the great Hindu epic, contains an extensive discussion on the importance of *ahiṃsā*. The following passages attest to the significance of *ahiṃsā* within the Hindu context :

> One should never do that to another which one regards as injurious to one's own self. This, in brief, is the rule of *dhamma.* yielding to desire and acting differently, one becomes guilty of *dhamma.*[18]

> The meat of other animals is like the flesh of one's son. That foolish person stupefied by folly, who eats meat, is regarded as the vilest of human beings.[19]

> Those high bound persons who desire beauty, faultlessness of limbs, long life, understanding, mental and physical strength, and memory, should abstain from acts of injury.[20]

> *Ahiṃsā* is the *dhamma.* It is the highest purification. It is also the highest truth from which all *dhamma* proceeds.[21]

> *Ahiṃsā* is the highest *dhamma:*
> *Ahiṃsā* is the best authority (*tapas*).
> *Ahiṃsā* is the greatest gift.
> *Ahiṃsā* is the highest self control.
> *Ahiṃsā* is the highest sacrifice.

Ahiṃsā is the highest power.

Ahiṃsā is the highest friend.

Ahiṃsā is the highest truth.

Ahiṃsā is the highest teaching.[22]

In these passages from the *Mahabhāratā*, *ahiṃsā* is described as the best action, giving birth to righteousness or *dhamma* and serving as the best possible means for purification.

In the classical Yoga System, which in a certain sense may be regarded as the premier renouncer school of the Hindu tradition wherein the values and some practices of the Jainas and the Buddhists are given sanction within the framework of orthodoxy, *ahiṃsā* is mentioned as the basis of and the reason for all ethical practices. The commentator Vyāsa defines *ahiṃsā* as being the absence of injuriousness (*anābhidroha*) towards all living beings (*Sarvabhūta*) in all respect (*Sarvathā*) and for all time (*Sarvadā*). It is said to result in the alleviation of enmity in the proximity of the one practising *ahiṃsā*.[23] Vyāsa acknowledges that circumstantial exigencies might preclude total practice of *ahiṃsā*. He gives examples of several cases in which one may be exempted from the practice of *ahiṃsā*. The first is that of the fisherman who only injures fish for his own survival. The second is the vow to abstain from killing only in a special place. *Ahiṃsā* here is required as the foremost spiritual dispelling to be strictly adhered to by aspiring yogis.

Non-Violence lies at the root of select forms of spiritual practice in all religious traditions. Regardless of religious distinctions, non-violent action also presumes that another person is, in a fundamental sense, not different from oneself. Philosophically, non-difference of self from others provides a theoretical basis for performing non-violence. The non-violent act provides an important step towards direct perception of the sacredness of all life. It serves to free one from restricted notion of self and sensitivity towards the wants and needs of other persons, animals and the world of the elements, all of which exist in reciprocal dependence.

In Hindu mythology, frequent occurrences of

transformations of humans into animals and vice versa show the recognition that animal life is as valid as, and thus interchangeable with, human life. The Hindu theory of transmigration of the soul accepts the logic that a soul taking births into several forms may take animal forms as well as human. So, the position of humans and animals are interchangeable when circumstances demand, or *kamma* (consequence of deeds from previous lives) dictates. In the story of *Dasāvatāra* (the ten incarnations), Lord Vishnu himself takes several births into animal forms before taking the human ones. It is significant that Hindus do not find it hard or unnatural to think of their God in animal forms. If their God himself can take up the humble forms of a fish (aquatic), a tortoise (amphibian), a boar (terrestrial) and a lion-man (half animal-half human), before human forms, it shows the kind of regard or reverence Hindus feel towards animals. There are also other areas of human indebtedness to animals recognised by Hindu scriptures. References have been made to animals' knowledge of medicinal properties of herbs. In the *Atharvaveda*,[24] where various plants are invoked to cure human ailments, mention is made of individual plants being known to boars, hawks, eagles, swans, birds and wild beasts. The cow is considered a holy animal in Hindu mythology. The cow is even worshipped in some parts of India on an auspicious day called *Gosthastame.* R. Pannikar is of the view, "Whatever origin or value we may ascribe to the sanctity and worship of the cow in India, the fact remains that for a predominantly agricultural civilization the worth of the cow cannot easily be overestimated".[25]

The Aryans enjoyed the meat of sacrificial animals. There are references which show that, in vedic culture, great honour was shown to a guest by offering young calf's meat for his meal (e.g. in *Uttara Rāmacharita* it is mentioned that the sage Vaṣiṣṭha was served veal in the hermitage of the sage Vālmiki), though they seem to have admired the cow as a very useful animal. The ideals of vegetarianism and non-violence developed under the influence of Buddhism and Jainism, though the first seeds of non-violence were sown in the Upaniṣads. The Upaniṣadic concept of all living creatures being part and parcel of *Brahma* emphasises the sacredness of all forms of life, and thus the killing of animals is unjustifiable. K.M. Sen[26] points out that the Vedic interest in gods had by then been replaced by interest in humanity and in human greatness. A strong sense of love and compassion for animals and other sub-human species led to vegetarianism. The fact that animals were treated compassionately in Hindu society is documented by the 16th century English traveller, Ralph Fitch, who came across a veterinary hospital in Cooch Bihar, as quoted by K.M. Sen[27] :

"I went from Bengal into the country of Couche.
Here they be all gentiles and they will kill nothing.
They have hospitals for sheep, goats, dogs, cats,
birds, and for all other living creatures. When
they be old and lame, they keep them until they die.
If a man catch or buy any sick thing in
other places and bring it thither, they will give
him money for it or other victuals, and
keep it in their hospitals or let it go".

This shows that social or public service was not restricted to humans in Hinduism but was extended to other living creatures also. The continuation of the same trend can be noticed in the preachings of Swami Vivekananda, the Hindu visionary and social reformer, at the turn of the 19th century (1863-1902) :

"Where do you seek your God,
overlooking Him in various forms, in front of you?
He serves God best.
Who is kind to all His creatures.

Attitude Towards Animals in Jainism

Jainism is one of the most ancient of India's traditions and the oldest of the surviving non-vedic schools. The practice of *ahimsā,* referred to in Jaina texts as non-injury or in other words "absence of the desire to kill or harm", is the heart of jainism. This is the prime practice in Jainism for overcoming past actions, and all dimensions of the religion and the philosophy including its logic, reflect a concern for *ahiṃsā*. Acts of violence are to be avoided because they will result in injury to oneself at some future time, even perhaps in another embodiment.

Lord Mahavira propounded five principles for his followers of which *ahiṃsā* is one of the greatest. *Ahiṃsā* is the main principle and is given first place. According to Sri Sruta Suri,[28] truth etc. are meant to support this main vow-*Ahiṃsā*, just as another is required to help the growth of grain, etc. Here *ahiṃsā* is defined as opposite to *himsā* where *himsā* means to separate the ten vitalities[29] by a *pramatta* (a careless person).[30] (*Pramatta* means that person who acts thoughtlessness he who intends to practice *ahimṣā* cunningly on account of strong promotion). In order to uphold the vow of *ahiṃsā*, two paths of practicc were developed. One for the Jaina monks, who adḥered to greater vow (*mahāvrata*) and another for the Jaina laymen, who followed a less uniform discipline (*Anuvrata*). These *Anuvratis* include non-violence (*ahiṃsā*), truthfulness (*Satya*), non-stealing (*astaya*), sexual restraint (*Brahmacarya*) and non-possession (*aparigrāha*). Four types of violence are acknowledged which are intention, non-intentional, related to profession and self defence. The Jaina monks live according to the rules that avoid all types of violence, while laymen are allowed to take life in some cases. All Jainas are strict vegetarians, living solely on one sensed beings (vegetables) and milk products. Alcohol, honey and certain kinds of fig can also be prohibitcd because they are said to harbour many forms of life, especially *nigoda* (micro organisms).

Ahiṃsā is said to be practised by the Jaina population, both lay and monastic, in five ways which are[31] :

(i) Restraint of mind (*Manogupti*)

(ii) Control of tongue (*Vacangupti*)

(iii) Carefulness on roads (*Iryasamiti*)

(iv) Removing beings from roads (*Adanānikṣepana Samiti*) and

(v) Eating in day-light to avoid ingesting bugs (*Alokita*

panabhojana Samiti).

In order to observe these forms of *ahiṃsā*, obedience to several rules is prescribed to uphold *anuvrata*, including care in movement, speech, eating, placing, removing and elimination. A rule suggests that one limit the area of one's activities, thus renouncing potential harm one may cause in far off places. This rule contributes to the regional nature of Jainism and monks face strong prohibitions against travel. These concerns have led the Jaina community to pursue limited means of livelihood. Government jobs and farming are acceptable but not desirable. Occupations like writing, arts and crafts are encouraged and commerce is the most desirable one, provided that the trade is not conducted in tools of violence, such as weapons.

As evidenced by these prohibitions, the world view of the Jainas presents an unparalleled concern for life. "All beings are fond of life, they like pleasure and hate pain, shun destruction and like to live, they long to live. To all, life is dear". With this view of life, we can say that Jaina community has exerted a great deal of influence on Indian society as a whole, though it has consistently remained a tiny minority. They have protested vigorously against the Hindu practice of animal sacrifice. One of the Jaina texts declares : "Those terrible ones who kill animals under the guise of making an offering to the gods or the guise of sacrifice, are bereft of compassion and go to bad fate". Largely as a result of their efforts, vegetarianism is practised in all parts of India, and animal sacrifice is now illegal in most areas.

One story which amply demonstrates the Jaina belief that animals can exhibit remarkable powers of both intellect and will goes thus :

"Long ago, there was a forest fire, and all the animals of this forest fled and gathered around a lake, including a herd of elephants, deer, rabbits, squirrels etc. The animals crowded together in their small refuge. The leader of the elephant herd got an itch and raised a leg to scratch himself. A tiny rabbit quickly occupied the space vacated by the elephant's foot. The elephant, out of an overwhelming desire not to hurt the rabbit, stood on three legs for more than three days until the fire died down and the rabbit simpered off. By then the elephant's leg was numb and he toppled over. Still retaining a pure mind and heart, the elephant died. As a reward for his compassion he overcame the need for embodiment as an animal and was born as a prince by the name of Megha and eventually became a disciple of Mahārājā, taking the vows of a monk in the hope of transcending all forms of existence."

This fanciful story is noteworthy for its confidence in animal abilities, illustrating the Jaina conviction that animals can hold a very high place in the greater order of things.

In Jain traditions we find too many instances where they advocate protection of animal life. We come to know from some Jaina texts that Jainas respect the life of even the smallest creatures. One text enjoins that one should after having listened to the doctrine of *Ahiṃsā*, give up at least *himsā* towards mobile beings, if one cannot also renounce *hiṃsā* towards immobile beings.[32]

There are various rules prescribed to regulate *ahiṃsā* in Jainism. *Iryasamiti* means care in walking so that no living beings such as insects, are killed. A saint who walks upon a frequented path, free from creatures, during the day time all the while carefully watching the ground at a distance of two yards ahead—he is observing care in walking.[33] Another rule is *āsana samiti* which means care in eating. One who takes food not specially prepared for him, which is free from living beings and offered by another with devotion—he is said to observe care in eating.[34] A monk should be careful when lifting things up and while putting them down (*adāna-nikssepana samiti*).[35]

There is a tendency in Jaina ethics to count each life unit as one. Although the texts distinguish between one, two, three, four and five sensed beings, in moral practice it is attempted to give the same value and justification for existence and enjoyment of the necessities of life to all living beings.

Attitude Towards Animals in Islam

The message of Islam is primarily addressed to human beings, instructing them how to obey God, communicating to them the joys of complying with His commands, and the penalties of disobedience. Islam believes in a harmonious relationship between human beings and the natural world. According to the Qurān, "There is not an animal on earth, nor a bird that flies on its wings—but they are communities like you... and they shall all be gathered to their Lord in the end".[36] This means that they fulfil the plan which God has allotted to them in his purpose. They are not to be treated as valueless by human beings. It has not usually been taken by the commentators of the Qurān to mean that animals share the bliss of life after death. Human beings are distinguished from animals by their capacity to make moral judgements. Only they, of all species of life, can choose to obey or disobey God, and so earn paradise or hell.

By going through Islamic literature one could say that Islam is not a sentimental religion. By God's permission, human beings have power over animals, as over all creation, and they can be used for various purposes :

> "He has created cattle for you. You get
> from them warmth and many benefits,
> and food. And you drive them
> home at night, and lead them to pasture
> in the morning. They carry your burdens
> to lands you could not reach except
> with great trouble. Your Lord is full
> of kindness and mercy. There are horses,
> mules and donkeys, for you to ride or for show".[37]

From the above passage one can draw the conclusion that the emphasis is put on the practical use of animals, but the last part indicates that some animals may be kept to give pleasure. Islam forbids the keeping of some animals for domestic purposes. That is why most of the Muslims do not have dogs as their pet animals. According to traditions of the Prophet, he ordered killings of dogs in Madināh, and warned that anyone who kept dogs other than to protect property or hunt would have good works debited from his balance sheet by God. This would count against him on the Day of Judgement.[38] The Prophet did not like dogs. He is reported to have said; "Were dogs not a species of creatures I should command that they all be killed, but kill every pure black one".[39] However, he did not mean that dogs could be mistreated. A prostitute who saw a thirsty dog hanging around a well one day, gave it water to drink. For this act of kindness, the Prophet pardoned all her sins. Conversely, a woman who had tied up a cat and not provided it with food or drink until it died was thrown into hell.[40]

Other traditions of the Prophet forbid treating animals cruelly. They are not to be caged or beaten unnecessarily or branded on the face, or allowed to fight each other for human entertainment. Animals should not be mutilated while they are alive, which forbids vivisection. Battering farming is not allowed to Muslims, so they are opposed to it and the slaughter of calves for veal, and all forms of animal husbandry which are cruel to creatures or which needlessly kill them. These interdicts arise out of the Islamic emphasis that human beings have a moral obligation towards animals.

But we also find some instances where the Prophet allowed hunting of animals for the purpose of food. The Prophet once said, "If anyone kills a sparrow or anything greater wrongfully, God will question him about killing it. On being asked what the night way was, he replied, "To cut his throat and eat it, but not cut off his head and throw it away".[41]

Islamic laws declare some things as permissible (*halāl*) for human beings and some other things as harmful *(haram)*, covering all aspects of life, which includes what should be eaten by human beings and what not. There are four forbidden categories of food which should not be eated by any devout Muslim, which are derived from the *Qurān* (5:4) :

(i) Meat of dead animals

(ii) Blood

(iii) Pig's flesh

(iv) Meat over which another name than God's has been invoked.

Other than these four categories, all types of food can be eaten and enjoyed by the Muslim and in doing so, no sin is done.

Islam along with Judaism and Christianity is a member of the larger category of abrahamic religious traditions. This group of traditions is dominated by an ethical anthropocentrism, although the human-centredness of each tradition is modified by important insights into the moral dimension of (i) other animals' lives and (ii) humans' instrumental use of other animals.

In Islamic tradition, much emphasis is given to the importance of humans as the centre of the universe, with other animals having been put here for their benefit. But recognition of a moral dimension of other animals as well as in human treatment of creatures who are deemed creatures of Allāh, does play an important role in the tradition. For example, there are passages in the principal Islamic scriptures, the *Qurān*, as well as in other important writings of the tradition such as the *Hadisa* and the *Shariāh* that recognize that other animals are not solely for human use and have their own importance as Allah's creatures.

Prophet Mohammad himself commented "who-ever is kind to the creatures of Allāh, is kind to himself"; and he compared the doing of good or bad deed to other animals with similar acts done to humans. Other animals might be said to have a high profile in the tradition, for there are many *Surahs* (chapter in the *Qurān*) named after animals.

Negative views about other animals appear in some Quranic passages : negative views that appear in the belief of various sects that infidels after death become other animals or that hell is full of noxious non human animals. The practice of public, ceremonial slaughter of other animals for food, which occurs on the last day of Ramzān, the traditional month of fasting and at other times when the meat is used for a celebrative feast and distributed to the poor, reflect the basic belief that humans are the vice-regents of Allāh and other animals are for their use. Rules designed to make the killing more human moderate the metamessage that humans are the only animals that really matters.

It is difficult to find bases for the rights of animals in the Islamic tradition because its perception of the moral norm of the universe has been interpreted in such an anthropocentric manner. Islamic ethics are based on two principles, the first of which is a general understanding of human nature and the second a combination of religious and legal grounds. Because the Islamic tradition's fundamental ethical values are held to be revealed, accurate and unalterable, the mechanisms that are available to foster acceptance of the increasing knowledge about perceptions of other animals' lives and abilities are not yet well developed. The existing pattern of reasoning continues to start from the view that it is humans who really matter.

Protection of animals in Islam is directly associated with values. The teaching of mercy is an essential part of the faith of Islam. The *Qurān* constantly stresses the mercy of God to man, and man is thus taught to show love and kindness to his fellows.[42] The *Qurān* not only discourages the killing of animals for mere fun and sport, but also enjoins kind treatment of them. It says, "there is neither an animal on the earth nor being that flies on the wings, they are communities like you". These are some of the instances discussed in the Islamic traditions which shows their eagerness towards animal protection and human treatment meted out to them.

Now-a-days, ritual killing of animals is condemned by many non-Muslim individuals and groups. The bottom line for Muslims is that it is commanded by Allāh and this order counts far more than the opinions of others. It is quite clear that Muslims are not mawkish about such matters. Since Islam began on the fringes of the desert, where staying alive was the most important concern of the people than any other thing, animal flesh was regarded as a necessity and not a luxury. Most of Muslim populace today live in relatively poor countries where survival counts more than middle-class values, which may seem excessively indulgent. So, in the end I am in a position to conclude that Islam gives human beings power over, and responsibility for, animals, who should be treated with kindness and considerations, but which by Allāh's permission, provide food, clothing and transport.

Attitude Towards Animals in Judaism

Kindness towards animals features prominently in the Jewish tradition. The ten commandments include domestic animals in the Sabbath rest : "Remember to keep the *Sabbath* day holy... you shall not do any work, you, your son or your daughter... your cattle".[43] Early in the 3rd century AD., the *Rabbis* formulated the 'Seven Laws for the Children of Noah', which was an attempt to define the religious obligations of human kinds in general, for all people are descended from Noah.

The laws which were unknown in this form in sources earlier than the 3rd century are as follows :–

(i) Do not blaspheme
(ii) Do not worship idols
(iii) Do not murder
(iv) Do not commit adultery
(v) Do not steal
(vi) Do establish court of justice
(vii) Do not eat 'a lamb torn from a living animal'.

The last of these laws covers cruelty to animals, evidently understood as a major human responsibility.

Pious tales and folklore exemplify this attitude in its literature. One of the tales is : "A calf was about to be slaughtered. It ran to Rabbi (Judha the Patriarch, about the year 200), nestled its head in his robe and whimpered. He said to it, 'Go! This is what you were created for!" As he did not show it mercy, heaven decreed suffering upon him. One day Rabbi's housekeeper was sweeping the floor. She came across some young weasels and threw them out; He said, 'Let them alone! It is not written, His mercies extend to all his creatures.' Heaven decreed, 'since he is merciful, let us show him mercy'.

Causing pain and distress to animals is also discussed in great detail in the Rabbinic laws. In the Rabbinic law, this concern condenses into the concept of 'Distress to living creatures'.[44] An illuminating instance of *halakhic* concern for animal welfare is the rule attributed to the 3rd century B.C. Babylonian Law that one should feed one's cattle before breaking bread oneself and even the *Sabbath* laws are relaxed somewhat to enable rescue of injured animals or milking of cows to ease their distress. The Torah does not enjoin vegetarianism, but restricts meat eating. Restrictions on meat eating perhaps indicate that it is a concession to human weakness. Joseph also, a medieval Jewish philosopher, wrote that the first people were forbidden to eat meat because of the cruelty involved in killing of animals.[45] Although the Torah does not insist on vegetarianism, it places considerable restraints on the eating of meat. Only the meat of certain type of animals may be eaten also certain parts of animals may be eaten and certain parts may not be eaten, and the blood must be drained. There are regulations as to how animals should be slaughtered. *Shehitah*, the method of slaughter, is by a single sharp cut across the trachea and esophagus and this may be performed only by a qualified religious expert. Now-a-days, there are special pens and procedures to ensure that the animal suffers the minimum of psychological distress and minimum pain. From time to time voices are heard suggesting that the *Shehitah* is cruel to animals, but the criticism often concerns un-essential aspects of *Shehitah*, such as the form of casting-pen used, rather than *Shehitah* itself.

However, Judaism does not recognise kindness to animals as an absolute value because Judaism consistently values human life more than that of any other living creatures. However, it stresses the special responsibility of human beings to look after other living creatures.

REFERENCES

1. Yajura Veda, 13.47.
2. O.P. Dwivedi, p. 203.
3. K.W. Morgan—*The Religion of the Hindus,* (New York, Ronald, 1943), p. 102.
4. *Yajurveda,* 13.49.
5. *Yajnavalkaya Smṛti,* Acārādhyaya, V, p. 180.
6. *Chhandogya Upanishad, 8.5.1.*
7. Manusmriti, 2.159.
8. Ibid., 5.43.
9. Ibid., 5.44.
10. *Śānti Parva* of the *Mahābhārata,* 15.49.
11. *Manusmṛti,* 5.41.
12. *Śānti Parva* of the *Mahābhārata,* 32.13.
13. *Śankara on Vedānta Sutra,* 3.1.25 and 3.4.28.
14. *Shānti Parva,* 215.7-8.
15. *Matsya-Purāna,* 108.20-21.
16. *Bhāgvata-Purāṇa* 10.51.63.
17. *Varāha* Purāṇa, 8.26-30.33.
18. *Mahābhārata,* II XI. 113.8.
19. *Māhābhārata.* XIII. 114.11.
20. *Mahābhārata.* XIII. 115.8
21. *Mahābhārata.* XIII. 125 : 25.
22. *Mahābhārata.* XIII. 115 : 41.
23. *Yoga Sutra.* 11:35.
24. *Atharvaveda.* VIII. 7:23-4.
25. R. Pannikar, *The Vedic Experience–Mmantra Manjare : An Anthology of the Vedas for Modern Man and Contemporary Celebrations.* (2nd edition), 1979, p. 286.
26. K.M. Sen, *Hinduism* (8th edn.) London, Penguin Books (1973), p. 64.
27. Ibid., p. 25.
28. *Tattvartha Vṛtti's auther Tattvarthadigam Sutra commetary,* VII, 1.
29. Ten vitalities are five sources touch, taste, smell, right and hearing and exhaling.
30. *Tattvartha Vṛtti.* II. 13-14.
31. *Tattvartha Sutra.* VII. 4.
32. *Purusrtha-Ssiddhyupāya.* p. 75.
33. *Niyaṃsāra.* 4.61
34. Ibid. 4.63.
35. Ibid. 4.64.
36. The *Qurān.* 6: 38.
37. Ibid. 16:5-8.
38. A.II. Siddique (ed.), *Sahih Muslim,* Vol. 3 nos. 3809-29.

39. J.R. Robson, *Mishkat-al-Masibih*, vol. 2. p. 876.
40. A.K. Siddiqui (ed.), *Sahih Muslim*, vol. 4, nos. 5570-76.
41. J.R. Robson, *Mishkat-al-Masibih*, vol. 2, Lahore (1970), p. 874.
42. A. Hussain, *Spirit of Islam*, (Bombay, 1958), p. 12.
43. Exod. 20 : 10, NEB.
44. In B. Shabbat 128b it is suggested that this principle is of biblical status.
45. Sefer Ha-Iqqarim, 3:15.

CONCLUSION

At one time or another we have all made use of animals. Historically, animals have participated in the development of practically every aspect of human civilization—in war and peace, in work and at play, in love (companion animals) and hate (varmints), in life (biological experiments) and in death (pet cemeteries). Besides, we also eat them and animal byproducts can be found not only in the foods we eat and the clothes we wear, but also on the walls of our homes, in drawing rooms, in kitchens and bathrooms, in toiletries, in the cars we drive. Animals as pets have in many ways provided a relaxing buffer from stressful events, companionship, protection, unconditional, love and a sense of responsibility in a way that promotes physical and psychological wellness. A large majority of us out of ignorance and many wantonly abuse them and violate against them. Perhaps no area of human-animal behaviour is in more need of understanding than animal related crimes and deviance. Animals play a role in our literature, art and music, religion and folklore, verbal symbolism and vocabulary, fashion design and advertising, our holdings and toys and in children's stories. Animal are and have been used in sport, recreation and leisure activities. Animals have historically been involved in our work systems and continue to play a major role in many national and in our work systems and continue to play a major role in many national and intentional economies.

Though the concern for the plight of animals in India dates back to the Later Vedic period when the authors of some of the Upanisads criticised the cult of animal sacrifice, the Buddha was the first important religious leader in the history of the world who waged an organised and relentless campaign for the protection of sentient animals. *Ahiṃsā* is one of the most important tenets of Buddhism. However, through the curves and turns of history, this aspect of Buddhism has not been emphasized as much as it should have been. In order to understand the contribution of Buddhism in safeguarding animal rights, it is pertinent to know the differences between Animal rights and Animal welfare. Proponents of animal welfare seek to alleviate the sufferings of animals while they are being exploited without attempting to question the fundamental basis of whether it is acceptable to exploit animals in the first place. On the other hand, animal rights activists hold that both humans and animals have rights against exploitation. The Buddhist principle of *ahiṃsā* combined both the ideas of animal welfare and animal rights.

Buddhist texts like the *Jatakās* are replete with examples where animals are cared for. In Buddhism, love for animals is not sentimentality but true spirituality. The Buddha found a profound rapport with all living beings. Buddhism believes in the spiritual unity of all creatures. It exhorts humans to befriend them. The impact of Buddhist ideals can been seen in the works of Aśoka, the great Mauryan king of Magadh. Aśoka was greatly influenced by Buddhist ideal of *ahiṃsā*. He tried to curb violence against animals and exhorted his subjects to show consideration towards them. He enacted several laws that required kind treatment of animals. These included resticting meat consumption, curtailing animal hunting and establishing hospitals and roadside watering stations for animals. This is a fine example of state intervention in safeguarding of animal rights during the early Buddhist period and it can act as a guideline for modern day governments.

However, the Buddhist preaching of non-violence (*ahiṃsā*) is not without contradictions. The Buddha said that even for sustaining life animals may not be killed. On the other hand, he is quoted to have said that raw flesh and blood may be used in the case of disease. We also came across a Bodhisattva supplying meat for a coin. Buddhism touched non-violence only on the fringe and did not make a deep impact upon it, in the sense that killing of animals continued in full swing at least till the days of Aśoka. Except perhaps bringing about a decreases in the popularity of great sacrifices, in the other three fields, the Buddha appears to have met with negligible success. The main cause of the Buddhist philosophy of non-violence (*ahiṃsā*) being a failure was its being riddled with all sorts of contradictions. The following two reasons further limited its impact :

(i) The Buddha, the masses as well as the rulers did not want to give up these ways of ministering to their ambitions, pleasures and livelihood.

(ii) The Buddha was not a temporal ruler, hence he had no actual power to impose a body of restrictive regulations and penalties on the laity as he had on his monastic followers.

By the way, in its later phases together with Jainism and Vaiśnavism. Buddhism helped greatly in the advocacy of vegetarianism. By linking compassion for animals with religious merit, Buddhism encouraged people to respect animal rights. The Buddha showed a new path to human beings to take a new step towards a new vision of human planetary stewardship, which will become a reality only if we begin to make the right choice based upon the ethics of respect and reverence for all living creatures and upon *ahiṃsā*. Our attitude based upon the principles of *Mettā, Karunā* and *Ahiṃsā* will do much to heal the planet and ourselves in the process.

The struggle for animal rights is more a struggle within the self than the society. More than the society, man needs to change himself. At the moment our human world is based on the suffering and destruction of non-human beings. The ideals of Buddhism are more relevant in such a situation. By propagating compassion and respect towards animals, Buddhist ideas can prevent abuse and exploitation of animals.

Equality of consideration is the theme of Buddhism which the Buddha himself talks about. Our present attitude towards animals is based on a long history of prejudice and arbitrary discrimination. There can be no reason except the selfish desire to preseerve the privileges of the exploiting group for refusing to extend the basic principle of consideration to other living beings. The basic principle of equality does not require equal or identical treatment but it requires equal consideration. This means that our concern for others and our readiness to consider their interests ought not to depend on what they are like or on what abilities they may possess. Just as we are concerned about a child to learn to read and write, the concern for the well-being of a pig may require no more than that we leave him alone with other pigs in a place where there is adequate food and room to run freely. The basic element of taking into consideration the interests of a being, whatever these interests may be, must be extended to all beings, black or white, male or female, human or non-human.

We are in a position to say that animals have occupied an important place in Buddhism and its literature. The *Jātakas* or the stories of the Buddha's former lives, include stories connected with previous lives of the Buddha who had taken birth in the form of animals. These stories illustrate the wisdom, the compassion and the moral behaviour manifested and exhibited by animals. These convey moral teachings that cruelty to animals for meat eating and sacrifice is not only unethical and irreligious but it threatens the very existence of human beings. There are two stories which I have come across in *Anguttara Nikāya* and *Vinaya Piṭaka* which throw great light on the position of animals in the early Buddhism. Through these stories the Buddha advises his lay followers and the bhikkhus to avoid hurting animals intentionally. In Buddhism, animals are not seen so much as animals but as potential humans or as animals that can teach humans some lessons. That is why animals occupy an important place in Buddhism.

Non-Violence or *Ahiṃsā* is the main theme of Buddhist philosophy. Buddhism appeals to human beings to follow the example of Cāra*vāka* bird that does no harm to any living creature and he earnest in the effort to lay aside the cudgel and the sword and be full of modesty, compassion and kindness to all creatures that have life. Even the minutest living beings did not escape from the notice of the Buddha. He ordered the monks to choose such places for the constructions of their houses where no living beings got injured or killed. Buddhism holds the fundamental precept of not taking life. Most of the Buddhist schools uphold the notion that animal life must be protected.

Buddhism was totally against the concept of meat eating. But the Buddha himself allowed meat in some cases. In the early Buddhist texts, it is found that the Buddha and his disciples used to eat meat but on the condition that they had not seen, nor heard nor had any suspicion that the meal was prepared especially for them. This condition in Buddhism is known as the *Rule of Tikotiparisuddha.* The Buddha listed animals whose meal could be eaten and also those whose flesh should not be eaten.

The Buddha was totally against animal sacrifice performed by the brahmanas because he was of the view that it did not achieve the objectives the brahmanas hoped for. Such criticism of animal sacrifice led to a great decrease in the use of animals in this way. The Buddha praised the brahmanas of old for not sacrificing animals and in *Kutādanta Sutta* its is explained that in a sacrifice which he had himself conducted for a king in his past life, no animals were killed, no trees were felled to act as sacrificial post, workmen were not forced to help and the only offerings were items such as butter and honey. The Buddha was of the opinion that to undo the effect of any bad actions, animal sacrifice was not the remedy. It would on the contrary only double the evil effect.

In the early Buddhist monastic code, monks were allowed to release trapped animals or fish, if this was from compassion rather than a desire to steal. A *Jātaka* story tells of the Bodhisattva, who as a hermit, during a drought, enssured that wild animals got water. In doing so, he was so busy that he had no time to garner food for himself, so that the animals gathered it for him in gratitude.

The most important qualities that human beings share

with animals are life and sentience. The capacity to suffer is the crucial similarity between human beings and animals that binds us all together and places us all in a similar moral category. Millions of animals every year are used in schools and universities for educational purposes. One of the greatest cruelties in medical research is the deliberate infliction of burns on animals. With so many tragic cases of burns victims in the wards of hospitals around the world, it seems totally unnecessary to inflict suffering on sentient animals. Vivisection should be stopped so that animals no longer suffer and die in laboratory experiments. Factory famring is quite a common phenomenon in the modern world whereas Buddhism is against unnatural production of this kind. Buddhism is also against the keeping of pet animals because it restricts their freedom by uprooting them from their natural environment. Human morality must expand to acknowledge and respect the rights of non-human animals. If human animals have rights, such as the right to life, so do non-human animals.

To prevent most of today's suffering by animals would require "radical changes in our attitude towards treatment of animals which would involve our diet, our approach to wildlife, hunting and trapping like circuses, rodeos and zoos". Most of the animals are aware of their environment, have beliefs and desires, possess memory and expectations about the future, and are able to act intentionally in seeking to fulfil their desires or purposes. Tom Regan, a prominent animal rights activist, is of the view, "No reasonable person would deny that the death of any animals would change the ecological balance". Some of the rights the animals must have are :

(i) All animals are born with an equal claim on life and the same rights to existence.

(ii) All animals are entitled to respectful treatment. Humanity as an animal species shall not arrogate to it self the right to exterminate or exploit other species. It is humanity's duty to use its knowledge for the welfare of animals. All animals have the right to attention, care and protection of humanity.

(iii) No animals should be ill treated or be subject to cruel acts.

(iv) All wild animals have the right to liberty in their natural environment and should be allowed to procreate. Deprivation of freedom, even for educational purposes, is an infringement of this right.

(v) Animals traditionally living in a human environment have the right to live and grow at the rhythm and under the condition of life and freedom peculiar to their species. Any interference by humanity with this rhythm or these conditions for purpose of gain is an infringement of this right.

(vi) All companion animals have the right to complete their natural life span. Abandonment of an animal is a cruel and degrading act.

(vii) Animal experimentation involving physical or psychological suffering is incompatible with the rights of animals, whether it be for scientific, medical, commercial or any other form of research. Alternative methods must be developed and used.

(viii) No animal should be exploited for the amusement of humanity Exhibitions and spectacles involving animals are incompatible with their dignity.

(ix) Any act involving wanton killing of animals is biocide, i.e., a crime against life.

(x) Any act involving mass killing of wild animals is genocide i.e. a crime against the species.

These rights of animals can be protected only through the Buddhist philosophy of *ahiṃsā* and other Buddhist principles. We know that the boundless kindness of the Buddha was directed not only to all human beings but to the dumb animals as well. It was the Buddha who banned animal sacrifice and admonished his followers to extend their loving kindness (*Mettā*) and *Karunā* to all living beings, even to the tiniest creature that crawls. No man, he taught, has the right to destroy the life of another as life is precious to all. A Bhikkhu is expected to exercise this loving-kindness to such an extent that he is forbidden by the *Vinaya* rules even to dig or cause to dig the ground. He cannot even drink water without it being filtered. Aśoka, the greatest Buddhist king, had this inscribed on a monolith : "The living must not be nourished with the living. Even chaff with insects must not be hurt".

A genuine Buddhist must practise this *Mettā* towards every living being and identify himself with all, making no distinctions whatever. It is this Buddhist *Mettā*, one of the most salient characteristics of Buddhism, that attempts to break all the barriers of caste, colour and creed which separate one man from another. Each living creature is as attached to its life as any other. In institutions such as Society for the Prevention of Cruelty to Animals (SPCA) and in sayings such as 'she is so kind, she wouldn't kill even a fly', we see that the notion of non-harming non-human life forms often extends to western culture too. Thus, Buddhism reaffirms some of our own cultural ideals.

Buddhism holds life to be one and therefore sacred. They do not, therefore, kill for sport. Killing sentient beings, including slaughtering of animals for food, is counted among the heaviest transgressions in Buddhism. This is not only because such acts create untold pain and suffering but also because they cut short the lives of the future Buddhas (as all sentient beings have a common Buddha-nature). Buddhist are of the view that animals have as much right to life as we on this earth that we share in common, and therefore we have no right to destroy them at our whim. Moreover, since in our ascent and descent on the ladder of innumerable lives, our Buddha-nature assumes many forms, to destroy any life form is to destroy a part of oneself. Buddhist are of the opinion that violence and warfare can never be ended as longas animal slaughter continues. It may not be out of place to quote Mahatama Gandhi, "The greatness of a nation and its moral progress can be judged by the way its animals are treated".

BIBLIOGRAPHY

Primary Sources (Textual Sources)

The Vinaya Piṭaka : Ed. H. Olderberg, 5, vols. London; PTS, 1879-1883. Tr. I.B. Homer; *The Book of the Discipline,* 6 vols. London; PTS, 1938-1966; tr. T.W. Rhys Davids & H. Oldenberg, *Vinaya Texts,* Vol. 13, 17, 20, SBE, repprint, Delhi : Motilal Banarasidass : 1982-85; Vinaya Pitaka (Hindi), Tr. Rahula Sanskritayan, reprinted and donated by the Corporate Body of the Buddha Education Foundation : Taipei : Taiwan.

The Digha Nikāya : Ed. T.W. Rhys Davids & J.E. Carpenter, 3 Vols. PTS, London, 1890-1911. Tr. T.W. & C.A.F. Rhys Davids; *The Dialogues of the Buddha;* 3 vols. 1899, 1910 & 1957 respectively (reprints), London; PTS.

The Majjhima Nikāya : Ed. V. Trencckner & R. Chelmers, 3. vols. London; PTS, 1888-1896. Tr. I.B. Horner; *The Collection of Middle Length Sayings,* 3 vols. London; PTS, 1954-1959 (Reprints).

The Anguttara Nikāya : Ed. R. Morris & E. Hardy, 5 vols. London; PTS, 1885-1900. Tr. F.L. Woodward; vols. I, II & V; E.M. Hare, vols. II & IV, *The Book of the Gradual Sayings,* London; PTS. 1955-1970 (Reprints).

The Samyutta Nikāya : Ed. M.L. Feer, 5 vols. London; PTS, 1884-1898. TR. C.A.F. Rhys Davids and S.S. Thera, Vol. I; C.A.F. Rhys Davids & F.L. Woodward vol. II; F.L. Woodward vols. III, IV, V. *The Book of the Kindred Sayings;* London; PTS, 1950-1956 (Reprints).

The Sutta Nipāta : Ed. V. Fausboll, London; PTS, 1885, Tr. K.R.

Norman; *The Group of Discourses,* with alternative Tr. by I.B. Horner & W. Rahula, London; PTS, 1984.

The Jātakas : Ed. V. Fausboll 7 vols. (7 vol. index by D. Anderson), Trubner & Co. London, 1877-1897. Tr. by various hands, 6 vols. Cambridge : Cambridge University Press, 1895-1907.

The Udānam : Ed. P. Steinthal, London; PTS, 1885. Tr. F.L. Woodward; **Verses of Uplift,** London; Oxford University Press, 1948.

The Theragāthā : Ed. K.R. Norman & L. Alsdorf; London; PTS, 1966. Tr. with an intro. & notes K.R. Norman; *Elder's Verses II*, London; PTS, 1969.

The Therīgāthā : Ed. K.R. Norman & L. Alsdorf; London; PTS, 1966. Tr. with an intro. & notes K.R. Norman; *Elders' Verses II,* London; PTS, 1971.

The Apādāna : Ed. M.E. Lilley; 2 vols., 1925-27, London; PTS.

The Itivuttaka : Ed. E. Wwindish; London; PTS, 1889, Tr. F.L. Woodward; *Itivuttaka : As It Was Said,* London; Oxford University Press, 1948.

The Petavatthu & The Vimānavatthu : Ed. N.A. Jayawickrama; London; PTS, 1977. Tr. H.S. Gehman; *Petavatthu; Stories of the Departed, The Minor Anthologies of the Pāli Canon,* Part IV, London; PTS, 1974. Tr. I.B. Horner (assisted by N.A. Jayawickrama); *Vimanavatthu; Stories of the mansions The Minor Anthologies of the Pāli* (Canon, Part IV, London; PTS, 1974).

The Mahā-Niddeśa : Ed. L. de le Vallee Poussin & E.J. Thomas; London; PTS, 2 Vols., 1916-17. Combined Reprint London; PTS, 1978.

The Culla-Niddeśa : Ed. A.C. Taylor; London; PTS, 2 vols., 1905, 1907. Tr. Bhikkhu Nxanamoli (with an intro. by A.K. Warder); *The Path of Discrimination,* London; PTS, 1982.

The Cariyāpiṭaka & The Buddhavaṃsa : Ed. N.A. Jayawickrama, London; PTS, 1974. Tr. I.B. Horner; *The Minor Anthologies of the Pāli Canon,* Part III, London; PTS, 1975. References are from R. Morris' edition, London; PTS, 1882.

The Dipavaṃsa : Ed. Tr. with intro. B.C. Law; *The Chronicle of the Island of Ceylon or the Dipavaṃsa,* Colombo : The Ceylon Historical Journal, 1959; 1-266.

The Mahāvaṃsa : Ed. W. Geiger; The Mahavaṃsa, London; PTS, 1908 & 1912. Tr. W. Geiger & M.H. Bode; *The Mahāvaṃsa or the Great Chronicle of Ceylon,* London; PTS, 1912.

The Manorathapurani : Buddhaghosa's commentary on the *Anguttara Nikāya,* ed. H. Walleser & H. Kopp, 5 vols, London; PTS, 1956-1973.

The Samāntapasādikā : Buddhaghosa's commentary on the *Vinaya Piṭaka,* ed. J. Takakusu & M. Nagai, 8 vols. (including index by H. Kopp), London; PTS, 1947-1975.

The Sumangala-Vilāsini : Buddhaghosa's commenary on the *Digha Nikāya,* ed. T.W. Rhys Davids, J.E. Carpentier & W. Stede, 3 vols. London; PTS, 1886-1971.

The *Sarattha-Pakasini* : Buddhaghosa's commentary on the *Samyutta Nikāya,* ed. F.L. Wwoodward, 3 vols., London; PTS, 1977.

The Maddhuratthavilāsini : Buddhadatta Thera's commentary on the *Buddhavaṃsa,* ed. & tr. I.B. Horner, London; PTS, 1946 & 1978.

The Paramāṭṭha-Dippaniudānaṭṭhakathā : Dhammapalacariya's commentary on the *Udāna,* ed. F.L. Woodward, London; PTS, 1977.

The Paramaṭṭhajotikāli : The *Sutta-Nipāta* commentary, ed. H. Smith, 3 vols., London; PTS, 1966-1972.

The Paramaṭṭha-Dipani : Dhammapala's commentary on the *Vimānavatthu,* ed. E. Hardy, Part IV; Dhammapala's commentary on the *Theragāthā,* ed. F.L. Woodward, 3 vols., London PTS, 1952-1956.

Dictionaries, Encyclopaedia etc.

Sanskrit-English Dictionary : Ed. M. Monier-Williams.

Pāli-English Dictionary : Ed. T.W. Rhys Davids & W. Stee, London; Pali Text Socieety; 1925.

Dictionary of Pāli Proper Names : Ed. G.P. Malalasekera, 2 vols., Reprint, New Delhi; Oriental Reprint; 1983.

Encyclopaedia Of Buddhism : First 6 vols., Colombo : Government of Ceylon; 1961-1996.

Encyclopaedia of Bioethics : Revised edition, Georgetown University, New York; Simon, Schuster and Micmillan; 1995.

International Encyclopaedia of Buddhism : Editor Narender Kumar Singh, Anand Publication Pvt. (Ltd.) New Delhi, 110021, 10 vols., Edition 1996.

Encyclopaedia of Animal Rights and Animal Welfare : Ed. Mare Bekoff (1998) Green Wwood Publishing Group Inc. USA.

Secondary Sources

Adams, Carol J., 1990 : *The Sexual Politics of Meat : A Feminist-Vegetarian Critical Theory*, New York, Continuum.

Aroson, H.B. : *Love and Sympathy in Theravāda Buddhhism*, Delhi, Motilal Banarasidass, 1980, 1996.

Banton, Miles; *Animal Rights*, New York; Gloucester Press; 1987.

Barnard, Neal D.; "Beyond the Draize Test : The Animals' Agenda, December, 1988.

Barua, B.M. *Aśoka and His Inscriptions*, Part II, Calcutta; New Age Publishers, 1965.

Barua, D.K., *"Buddhism and Lay Worshipers"*, Mahabodhi, LXXIV, Nos. 3-4 : 39-44.

Beauchamp, Tom L and Tom Regan (eds). 1993, *Matters of Life and Death : New Introductory Essays in Moral Philosophy*, 3rd edition, New York; McGraw-Hill.

Basham, A.L., *The Background to the Rise of Buddhism*, A.K. Narain (ed), Studies in History of Buddhism, Delhi, 1980.

Bechert, H. *Ethical Theory*, U.S.A. Eaglewood Cliffs, J.J.; 1989.

Besant, Annine; *Vegetarianism in the Light of Theosophy*, Madras; 1932.

Bhandarkar, D.R. *Aśoka*, Calcutta : Unversity of Calcutta, 1925.

Bryant, John; *Fettered Kingdoms*, Washington, DC. PETA, 1982.

Buchanan, Patrick; "Animal Rights and Ideology, "The Washington Times, 5 December, 1988.

Cartmill, Matt; "Animal Rights and Wrongs," *Natural History*, July 1986.

Carlson, Spence; "Animals are Victims of Vast Human-regulated System of Slavery," *Los Angeles Times*, 22 April 1987.

Chapple, C.K. *Nonviolence to Animals, Earth and Self in Asian Tradition*, First Indian Edition, New Delhi; Sri Satguru Publication 1995.

Chandra, Amulya, *Aîoka's Edicts*. The Institute of Inology, Calcutta, , 1956.

Darwin, C., *The Expression of the Emotions in Man and Animals*, New York; 1897.

Dolan, Edward F. JR.; *Animals Rights*, New York; Franklin Watts; 1986.

Eliade, M., *A History of Religious Ideas* (Vols. 1-3) (W.R. Traks. Trans.) Chicago Press.

Eliot, C.; *Hinduism and Buddhism*, London; 1954-6.

Fisher, James; *Zoos of the World : The Story of Animals in Captivity*, Garden City, NY : 1967.

Fleet, J.F. *"The Day on Which Buddha Died"*. JRAS, 1909; 1-334, 426-428.

Fox, Michael W. 1980, *Returning to Eden; Animal Rights and Human Responsibility*, New York; Viking Press.

Giehl, Dudley; *Vegetarianism : A Way of Life*, New York; Harper & Row; 1979.

Ghosh, I.M. *Ahiṃsā : Buddhist and Gandhian*, Delhi, Indian Bibliographies Bureau.

Griffin, Donald. R., *Animal Minds*, Chicago; University of Chicago; 1992.

Herscovici, Alan; *Second Nature : The Animal Rights Controversy*, Toronto : CBC Enterprises : 1987.

Horner, I.B. "*Early Buddhism and Taking of Life*", D.R. Bhandarkar, K.A. Nilakanta Sastri et.al. (eds), B.C. Law Volume, I, Calcutta; 1945.

Jasper, J.M. and Nelkin, D. (1992), *The Animal Rights Crusade : The Growth of a Moral Protest,* New York : The Free Press.

Jayatilleke, K.N.; *Ethics in Buddhist Perspective,* Wheel Pub. No. 175/176, Kandy : Buddhisst Publication Society, 1972.

Kapleau, R.P.; *To Cherish All Life : A Buddhist View of Animal Salughter and Meat eating,* The Buddha Educational Foundation, 1981.

Keown, D.; *Buddhism & Bioethics,* Britian Macmillan Press Ltd.

King, F. Wayne; "*Animal Rights : A Growing Moral Dilemma,*" Animal Kingdom, January-February, 1988 : 33-35.

Koshland, Daniel JR; "*Animal Rights and Animal Wrongs,*" Science, 10 March, 1989; 1253.

Linzey, Andrew, 1976, *Animal Rights : A Christian Assessment of Man's Treatment of Animals,* London, SCM.

Magel, Charles R. 1989; *Keyguide to Information Sources in Animal Rights,* Jefferson, NC; McFarland.

Mason, Jim and Peter Singer, 1990; *Animal Factories,* Revised edition, New York; Harmony.

McCoy, J.J; *In Defense of Animals,* New York; Seabury Press; 1978.

McDermott, James P. (1989); "*Animals and Humans in Early Buddhism,*" Indo-Iranian Journal, 32; 269-280.

Miler H. & W. Williams; *Ethics and Animals,* Clifton NJ. Humana Press.

Misra, G.S.P.; *Development of Buddhist Ethics,* Delhi, Munshiram Manoharlal.

Mookerji, Radhakumud, *Asokan Inscription : A Commentary.*

Morris, Richard Knowels and Michael W. Fox (ed); *On the Fifth Day : Animal Rights and Human Ethics,* Washington, DC; 1978.

Moulton, C.M. Kaufmann, & J. Filip; *Report on the Summit on*

Violence Towards Children and Animals, Englewood, CO; American Humane Association.

Moran, Victorian; *Compassion : The Ultimate Ethics*, Rochester, VT; Thorsons Publishing Group, 1985.

Nakamura, H. *"Ethical Values of Buddhism in Light of World Civilization"*, Berkeley Busei, 1958; 15-20.

Midgley, M. (1984), *Animals and Why They Matter*, Athens, (IA, University of Georgia Press.

Noske, Barbara, *Humans and Other Animals*, London; Pluto Press, 1989.

Nelkin, D. and Jasper, J. (1992), *The Animal Rights Controversy*, In; D. Nelkin (Ed.), Controversy; Politics of Technical Decisions, London, Sage.

Pacelle, Wayne; *"Biomachines : Life on the Farm Ain't What it Used to Be,"* Vegetarian Times, january, 1989.

Pande, G.C. *"On the Question of the Social Origins of Buddhism"*, Boddhi-Rasmi, New Delhi, Motilal Banarasidass, 1984.

Pande, G.C., *Studies in the Origins of Buddhism*, Allahabad : University of Allahabad, 1957.

Parham, Barbara; *What's Wrong with Eating Meat?* Denver; Anandarg Publication, 1979.

Prasad, C.S. "Meat-Eating and the Rule of Tikotparisudda", A.K. Narian (ed.), Studies in Pali and Buddhism, New Delhi : 1979 : 289-295.

Prasad, C.S. *"Logic Behind Allowing Meat-Eating and Prohibiting it in Buddhism"*, Transactions of the International of Orientalists, Japan, XVI, 1971 : 104f.

Pringle, Llaurence; *The Animal Rights Controversy*, San Diego; Harcourt Brace Jovanovich; 1989.

Quammen, David; *Animal Rights and Beyond : Natural Acts*, New York; Dell Publishing Co., 1985; 135-140.

Rajapakṣe, V. Journal of Buddhist and Pali University of Sri Lanka, Vol. 3.

Regan, Tom; *The Case for Animal Rights*, Berkeley; University of California Press; 1983.

Regan, Tom; *The Struggle for Animal Rights*, Clarke's Summit, PA; International Socieety for Animal Rights; 1987.

Rohr. Janelle (ed.); *Animal Rights : Opposing Viewpoints*, San Diego; Greenhaven Press; 1989.

Rollin, Bernard E.; *Animal Rights and Human Morality*, Buffalo; Prometheus Books; 1981.

Ruegg, D.S. *"Ahiṃsā and Vegetarianism in the History of Buddhism"*, Samaratna et.al (eds), Buddhisst Studies in Honour of Walpola Rahula, London, 1980.

Saddhatissa, H. *Buddhisst Ethics : Essence of Buddhism*, New York; G. Braziller, 1970.

Sarao, K.T.S., *"Meat-Eating and Non-Violence in Early Indian Buddhism"*, a paper presented at the 7th Conference of the International Association of Buddhist Studies, Bologna, Italy, 1985.

Sapontzis, Steve F.; *"Moral Community and Animal Rights,"* American Philosophical Quarterly, July 1985.

Sapontzis, Steve F. (1987), *Morals, Reason and Animals*, Philadelphia; Temple University Press.

Serpell, James A.; *In the Company of Animals*, Neww York; Basil Blackwell; 1986.

Singer, Peter (ed); *In Defense of Animals*, New York; Harper & Row, 1985.

Singer, Peter and Tom Regan; *Animal Rights and Human Obligations*, Eaglewood Cliffs, NJ; Prentice-Hall, 1976.

Smit-Chhristopher, D.L. (ed.) Subverting Hatred; *The Challenges of Nonviolencc in Religious Traditions*, Boston : Boston Research Centre for the 21st Century, 1998.

Stanley G. & Rosalind and Harris, J.; *Animals, Men and Morals : And Enquiry into the Maltreatment of Non-Humans*, London : Gollanez.

Story, F.; *The Place of Animals in Buddhism*, Kandy, BPS.

Tahtinen, Unto *Ahiṃs,* London, Rider and Company.

Thomas, E.J. *"Buddha's Last Meal"*, Indian Culture, Calcutta, XV, 1948.

Walli, K. *The Conception of Ahiṃsā in Indian Thought*, Varanasi, Bharata Manisha.

Index